MODI

LEADERSHIP, GOVERNANCE
and
PERFORMANCE

How to Order

This book is also available on special quantity discounts from the publisher Orient Publishing, 5A/8, Ansari Road, Darya Ganj, New Delhi - 110 002. Tel: +91-11-2327 8877, Fax: +91-11-2327 8879 email: mail@orientpaperbacks.com.

MODI

LEADERSHIP, GOVERNANCE AND PERFORMANCE

Vivian Fernandes

Foreword by
Raghav Bahl
Founder & Editor
Network 18

Orient Publishing
DELHI | MUMBAI | HYDERABAD

DEDICATION

To my beloved grandmother, who lived up to a few days short of one hundred years with humour, and my brother, who left us early.

ISBN : 978-81-222-0574-9

Modi: Leadership, Governance and Performance

Subject: Biography / Political / Leadership

© Vivian Fernandes

Cover Image © Rachit Goswami / Living Media India Limited

1st Published 2014

Published by
Orient Publishing
(an imprint of Orient Paperbacks)
5A/8 Ansari Road, New Delhi-110 002
www.orientpublishing.com

Cover Design by Vision Studio

Printed at
Saurabh Printers Pvt. Ltd., Noida

Cover Printed at
Ravindra Printing Press, Delhi-110 006

Contents

Foreword by Raghav Bahl

Preface

1. Compulsive Compaigner ~ 19
2. The Shield of Development ~ 49
3. New Charms for Agriculture ~ 73
4. Resetting Tribal Lives ~ 92
5. Chinese-style Implementation ~ 105
6. Opportunistically Inclusive ~ 120
7. Commerce Without Care? ~ 133
8. Modi on Kashmir and Foreign Policy ~ 144
9. What Drives Modi? ~ 147

Foreword

I have known Vivian Fernandes for nearly two decades, since the day he walked into TV18's fledgling news operations as a 'veteran' business journalist. He had built a fine reputation working with mainstream publications, while we were greenhorns trying to build a beach head for business journalism on the rather nascent medium of TV. Frankly, print titans virtually sneered at television news in the early 90s. It was seen as too flimsy, scratchy, using flowery adjectives to hide the lack of depth and substance. So we were delighted that somebody of Vivian's gravitas had jumped ship; we hoped to suck a bit of his reputation and credibility into our 'ephemeral journalism'.

Vivian had an unusual penchant for detail and enquiry. He would always buttress his assertions with facts. Rarely would he use an adjective without supporting it with relevant material. Now that amount of density works wonderfully in a 1000-word print article. On TV, it often becomes dreadfully incomprehensible. That's the first challenge Vivian had to confront. A 150-second, 150-word TV news 'package' was the norm; 1000 words were heretical. Details, so fulsome in prose, had to be intelligently, almost mercilessly, compressed for television copy. While Vivian gamely re-learnt the rules of the new game, I suspect he remains a bit unconvinced, to this day, twenty years out, on the need to crunch the copy so violently!

Over the years, I have seen two major transformations in Vivian's journalism (in a loose sort of way, my thoughts too have moved along similar trajectories). As with almost every strapping young professional in the early 90s, Vivian too was grappling with India's stalled leftward lurch. All of us had grown up under the umbrella of socialism and big government. Even if we were instinctively uncomfortable with such an ideology, we had no way of knowing anything better, since India had singularly avoided an alternate narrative. But all of that changed in the 90s. Suddenly, India was forced to embrace open trade, free markets, private enterprise, and the virtues of a small government. Many of us felt liberated — an ideology that lay invisibly, latently coiled within us, sprung forth with delighted conviction. Yes! That's what India needed to break through its debilitating poverty and under-development. Without quite knowing it then, many of us had shifted, from an involuntary left of center stance to a natural right of center advocacy. I suspect Vivian was one of those 'converts'.

The second transformation is the inexorable movement from intelligence to wisdom that many blessed people make as they grow older. From a reporter on policy issues, Vivian has today acquired the knowledge of an expert — from a beat guy he has become a policy wonk! In fact, he combines the best of both — he has a journalist's eye for arresting, breezy detail, which he can effortlessly weave into a 'near academic' output. I detected this evolution during the year Vivian spent researching and editing my book *Superpower?: The Amazing Race Between China's Hare & India's Tortoise*. We would have rather long, often agonized, debates about how India was deflecting away from its potential; how India's effete political leadership was squandering its destiny; how incremental and scared policy making was compromising our growth and security; how the rhetoric around poverty was actually keeping us poor; how a left-leaning and old-world political leadership had paralyzed India. Invariably, those debates would veer towards Chief Minister Narendra Modi's much talked about — extolled and derided in almost equal measure — 'Gujarat model of governance'.

Vivian, like many journalists, has had a chequered acquaintance with Mr Modi. But over the years, Vivian has developed a grudging admiration for what Mr Modi has achieved in Gujarat. Unlike other journalists, many of whom vacillate between blind admiration and visceral dislike, Vivian, hopefully, will be able to convince the reader about his trademark objectivity.

Vivian's core assertion is that those who cherish the rule of law and India's pluralism should not discredit Mr Modi's sensible economics and record of governance in their anxiety to attack political Hinduism (or Hindutva). The two must not be confused.

Alas, according to Vivian, Mr Modi does not make the grade in accommodating dissent or decentralizing power. Yet, Mr Modi gives officers long tenures and a free hand. He does not allow political interference in PSUs or transfers of officials. For Vivian, Mr Modi is a doer. He is great at execution. He supports innovative ideas. He learns on the job. He has been a disrupter. Perhaps his biggest challenge now would be to win the hearts of Muslims and modernize the community.

My best wishes to Vivian for his book.

Raghav Bahl
Founder & Editor, Network 18

PREFACE

So much has been said about Narendra Modi, can anything more be said about him? His life has been minutely chronicled. As a politician he is either admired or reviled. His economic achievements are extolled, defended or derided. His role in the 2002 riots has been scrutinized and his clearance by courts has been shown in a book, *The Fiction of Fact-finding*, published on the eve of the Lok Sabha elections to be the result of a special investigation team's cover up exercise.

There is little that Modi says or does that remains unknown. Modi is his own megaphone. Perhaps no other Indian politician on his side of the century has been as much in the public eye. Some see him as India's deliverer; others find him troubling. There are so many aspects to the man that he can take the shape of one's imagination.

It is true that Modi has failed to bring the criminals involved in the 2002 riots to justice. He does not tolerate dissent but few Indian leaders do so as a matter of principle. Muslims are alienated from his government, but he did not reach out to them till he stepped on to the national arena. Despite these faults, I believe that discrediting his economic achievements is no way to attack his politics.

Modi is pro-business, not necessarily pro-market. He is a liberalizer; a measured one. Unlike Prime Minister Atal Behari Vapayee's NDA government at the centre which went beyond disinvestment to actually selling off some state enterprises, Modi does not believe in privatization. Instead, he tries to make them profitable by giving bureaucrats a free hand, and keeping politicians away. But he is the only political leader who speaks loudly and consistently for private enterprise. He constantly exhorts youth to be job creators not job seekers. He is against the culture of entitlements and dependency. He is the most vocal articulator of minimum government, though this should not be confused with minimal government. Modi is no Tea Party Republican. He does not want to roll back the state, but he does not believe in bureaucratic creep either.

All this is anathema to the Leftists whose electoral prospects have shrunk considerably but occupy mind space far out of proportion to their political influence. They have not reconciled to the fact that their statist policies bankrupted India and drove industry out of whichever state they ruled. Unable to reinstate the public sector to the position it held before economic reforms were brought in, they want to make the terrain tough for private enterprise. Since they cannot deny that Gujarat has a high rate of economic growth, they question the quality of that growth. Pro-big business, jobless growth, heartless capitalism … these are some of the mock phrases used.

Gujarat has seen strong agricultural growth. Growth in agriculture reduces poverty much more than growth in other sectors. It would be wrong to term Gujarat's economic progress as benefiting only the moneybags. Nor is Modi's government blind to the state's underachievement in the social sectors. Over the past decade he has tried to catch up. There has been a vigorous enrolment drive. The number of schools has doubled. Most of them are government schools, unlike in Kerala. Students' attainments are not way off levels in other states — but that is poor consolation.

Modi is not unconcerned about high child malnutrition in Gujarat. The then managing director of a Baroda-based transport multinational, who was part of his business delegation, observed Modi inquiring from Nestle while on a tour of Europe in 2007, whether it could make nutritious candies for children from *bhal*, a variety of high-protein wheat grown in the state. Vitamin fortified candies are provided in *anganwadis*. However, the emphasis on private provision of healthcare, to make up for the lack of medical specialists in the government system, may be misplaced. It has attenuated an already weak public healthcare system. Markets do not work in healthcare. Patients lack bargaining power with doctors, due to the asymmetry of information. The design is flawed, but concern is not lacking. Nevertheless, Gujarat has made considerable progress. The infant mortality rate, for example, has fallen from sixty-four per thousand live births in 2001 to thirty-eight.

There is a Gujarat model of development, led by private enterprise which is different from the Tamil Nadu model, where private wealth creation is married to efficient public delivery of welfare. Regardless of their party affiliation, Gujarat's governments have consistently sought to attract investment into industry. Officials in charge of the industry portfolio belonged to a cadre within a cadre, with privileges like expense accounts, which were not available to colleagues in other ministries and departments. Gujarat was the first state in India to have an investor escort service. The denudation of industry in West Bengal following the Communist takeover, and the de-industrialization of Mumbai because of the prolonged, violent textile strike of the 1980s, brought industry to enclaves like Vapi in Gujarat.

While there is no Modi model of development, there is a unique Modi way of making it happen. Unlike chief ministers who allowed officials to be at the steering wheel of investment promotion, Modi leads from the front. After the riots this was as much a political compulsion as a personal necessity.

What magic has Modi performed? Haryana's economy has done as well without making as much fuss. Maharashtra, and Tamil Nadu are a step behind. In agriculture, Gujarat is a high performing state, but a few others have done better. There is no easy answer. If political stability, continuity of policies, ease of doing business and pro-active governance matter, then Modi's stewardship of the state would have had a levitating influence.

Modi is perhaps the only leader to have a philosophy of governance. He tries to make administration cohesive, ensures that it remains in touch with people through enforced campaigns and breaks down silo thinking by lifting critical programmes from the narrow confines of their departments for government-wide ownership.

Gujarat's development is Chinese in characteristics with its combination of (Hindu) cultural nationalism and economic development. There is a uncanny similarity between Modi wearing the mantle of Development Man soon after the 2002 riots, the Vibrant Gujarat investment summits, and the development of Shanghai's Pudong financial district as the 'dragonhead' of the Chinese economy after the Tiananmen massacre. Since Modi projects himself as the personification of Gujarat's development and embodiment of its pride, the distinction between person and the state is blurred. Corporates, building his image, or helping him politically, can pass it off as a patriotic duty. The media is abuzz about the alienation of public wealth to corporate favourites. Favours, when bestowed, are dressed up in an 'acceptable' package. Sometimes conscientious officials spoil the party. Yet, corporate avarice may not have been indulged. Which is why, Gujarat is seen as a relatively clean state. For all their financial power, corporate groups also do not have the heft to unmake Modi. They fear him.

With the political opposition defunct, and the Gujarati media behaving like poodles, Modi must thank Left liberals and the national media for acting as watchdogs and conscience keepers. With their relentless vigilance, human rights activists and some journalists have forced Modi to check the excesses of the Hindutva's loony fringe and focus on development. They have given a flicker of hope to the forlorn Muslim community and halted its slide into despair. They have ensured that the voice of the voiceless is not muffled by the drumbeat of development.

My first acquaintance with Gujarat was in 2008 when I was doing a series on governance for my own *Swantha Sukhay* or self-satisfaction. It was beyond my usual remit as economic policy editor of CNBC-TV18, a pioneering television channel devoted to stock market commentary and retail investment advice. While doing that programme, I met some motivated and well-meaning Gujarat officials, with whom I continue to be in touch. A television series on the state of our cities also brought me to Gujarat because Ahmedabad was the first city corporation in India to issue municipal bonds, which are still a rarity in India unlike in the United States.

In July that year, I interviewed Modi for the channel I was working for. The focus was entirely on development, The intention was not to gloss over Modi's politics, whose exclusivist Hindutva vision secular liberals like me cannot agree with, and I said so parenthetically while introducing the show. But I thought raking up the 2002 riots would only eclipse aspects of Modi's governance which the public should know to make an informed assessment of the man.

Thereafter I had occasion to meet Modi twice. Once, in November 2008, while moderating a debate at the inauguration of a Canadian metro coach manufacturer's factory near Baroda. Modi could not resist jabbing the Congress Party and its affinity to the Muslim community: 'Those who are interested in vote bank politics talk about bomb. I am interested in the politics of development so I talk of Bombardier.'

The second was in January 2012 when I was assigned to interview Modi soon after the Vibrant Gujarat investment summit. I was surprised at the invitation. I flew in and flew out. It was the shortest interview that never happened. The question he declined to take was innocuous. Some economists had ascribed Gujarat's agrarian 'miracle' under Modi to the vigorous check dam movement. But a few policy wonks from Hyderabad had questioned their assumptions. They said that Gujarat had seen higher agricultural growth in the 1990s. They disputed the role of rain water conservation. A string of successive good monsoons and the recharge of underground aquifers by the Narmada canal emptying into various rivers as it flowed northward were instead responsible they said. Gujarat's agriculture was still vulnerable to weather shocks they asserted.

What is your take on the issue? I asked Modi. I did not wish to send the questions in advance, but had relented. I thought I would get a considered reply. I was told by the PR executives not to ask the question, but I explained why I had to, and did.

Modi did not oblige. He could have answered it. Punctuality, they say, is the politeness of kings. Answerability to journalists, I suppose, is the politeness of chief ministers. Modi was under the mistaken impression that the interview was part of a paid marketing initiative for Vibrant Gujarat. Even if it is advertising, it is taxpayers' money. And even if the question were say, posed by a marketing executive and not a journalist, why should a chief minister decline to answer it, if it is not utterly stupid or offensive? Both are citizens equally. Not wishing to leave a mess behind, I told Modi I could skip the question and proceed with the interview. 'Why create bad blood,' I said. 'Bad *blood aapke dil me hai!*' came the reply, as Modi untangled the lapel mike and rose. I was amused at the incident and narrated it only to a few colleagues.

I also got a chance to research Gujarat extensively and travel through the state when the founder of Network 18 group of television channels, Raghav Bahl, appointed me as the executive editor of his book on India and China, which was published in the English-speaking world by Portfolio, an imprint of Penguin. He was generous enough to allow me to write chapters on Gujarat, Tamil Nadu and Andhra Pradesh, under my name. We called them India's Dragon States.

Early in 2013, I was once again in Gujarat. A fellowship from Delhi's Centre for Study of Developing Societies allowed me to travel through the tribal districts of the state and get acquainted with an innovative project of tribal uplift. The initiative fell short of its objective of doubling average tribal incomes over five years, but I came across many tribals who said they had profited. Government initiatives do not achieve their objective for several reasons. Often it is insincerity. That was not the case with this one. The secretary who had initiated it brought zeal to the endeavour and good management practices. He had a problem-solving attitude, which sadly, the people I met said his successor lacked. I am told that has now been corrected.

I do not believe in the journalism of negativity. The negative is often mistaken for the objective in my vocation. It has become the default position for many journalists because it is less demanding. If one is positive, one has to explain to avoid being perceived as 'sold out.' My intention is not to prettify either. I would rather say it as it is.

Saying it as it is, or observation-based journalism, sadly, is under assault now from the disintermediation of professional journalists by Internet technologies, and acute competition, as the sources of news have proliferated. News gathering budgets, always residual in Indian newspaper outlays, are shrinking. In news television, news gathering is a significant item of cost, but the money is spent on chasing eyeball-grabbing headlines, rather than understanding the underlying news and engaging the mind. Some of the top newspapers make humungous profits but their greed is insatiable. Ethics are discounted to the extent they can without seriously eroding credibility. They would rather lavish money on marketers and management mavens, than on reporters pounding the streets. Investigative journalism, by which I mean the thorough examination of the effectiveness of policies and programmes, and not just scandal-mongering, is still an individual journalist's enterprise; collective resources are seldom deployed.

In television channels, if you are not anchor material, your career chances are limited, no matter how good a reporter you are. The veterans among anchors have spent so much of their waking time in studios and away from the sun that it is an evolutionary mystery why they have not turned into the likeness of mushrooms in pigmentation. Sarcasm aside, reporting has become an endangered vocation and journalism, that infrastructure of democracy, is crumbling. This is why parties and candidates can make tall claims without fearing serious factual challenge.

I owe a ton of gratitude to Raghav Bahl, with whom I have been associated for two decades. I have seen him build a big business from just an idea and ambition — and have observed the pain, the ache, and the despair of entrepreneurship. Raghav has a nice way of drawing the best out of people. If something is reasonably good, he will say it is excellent. If it falls short of his standards, he will never say it is bad. Rather, he will say, 'can we meet for a conversation on this?' His book on China and India, was a journey of discovery for both of us (a paid one for me!). He has been very encouraging in this endeavour as well, and has given me a lavish introduction.

To Dr Jain I say thank you. His name is Peeyush and he is a cardiologist at a well-known heart institute in Delhi but I call him DJ, because he makes life music. His zest for photography and travel has brought us together. My photo on the back cover is a tribute to his talent. What age withers, DJ flatters!

I am grateful to Dhiren Avashia, Modi's long-time communications adviser, for sharing his insights. I fondly remember Hardev Sanotra for prodding me to go ahead when I was in two minds. Krishna Swamy for putting me in touch with my publisher, Sudhir Malhotra, who has been ever so ready, willing and quick. Much thanks to editor Deepa Mathur for smilingly trawling through my manuscript and improving it. I owe Himanshu Mehta and Vinod Harbola of Network 18's video tape library a nice meal. I thank my wife Glenda for letting me test my copy on her!

4 April, 2014   Vivian Fernandes

1. Compulsive Campaigner

Modi relies on mass drives to constantly renew his connection with people and keep his administration grounded. He is perhaps the only ruling leader with a philosophy of governance.

Modi is essentially a mobilizer. He loves campaigns not only during elections but also in between. Every year he charges up the administration with a new theme. If it is a Nirmal (sanitary) Gujarat one year, it is Nirogi Balak (healthy child) the next. Modi claims these programmes are not discrete, discontinuous events, but flow into each other. His intention is to make government function like a team and to secure the involvement of people in development. Cohesive administration and people's participation sum up Modi's governance style. Together, they add up to Team Gujarat.

In a 2008 interview, Modi said, '*mera ek mool bhoot* (fundamental) thinking *hai*. Until and unless you understand that philosophy you will not understand what I am doing.' Why did so many people give their lives for the freedom struggle? he asked. It is because 'Mahatma Gandhi converted the independence urge of individuals into a mass movement. My thinking is that development must be a movement.'

Speaking in Delhi at an event organised by a foundation which propagates free-market thinking, Modi said he believes in 4Ps or

'People Public Private Partnership model.' Evangelists for Modi's style call it P2G2 or Pro-Poor Good Governance.

'Until and unless you have people's participation you cannot give a result,' Modi said when I met him in his rather cold home-office in Gandhinagar, which was agnostic of any Gujarati motif. 'What is the meaning of democracy?' he asked. 'Go for a vote. Be in contract for a particular party or a particular person for a five-year term. I do not think that is true meaning of democracy.'

A government cannot deliver without the involvement of people. Modi gave the earthy example of state transport bus passengers tearing the rexine covers of seats and pulling out PVC foam to occupy themselves while travelling. The feeling of *'mujhe kya, mera kya'* must give way to good citizenship, or a sense of ownership which comes from belonging, he said.

Modi held up his model of governance as combining government's leadership with people's involvement. 'Government is all and sole, I do not believe,' he said. 'My motto is minimum government, maximum governance.'

Mass leaders derive their power and authority from people. The irony in Modi's case is that he is said to be a loner. He has no ties of family having broken off at a young age. Reports say that he has associates and followers but few friends. Perhaps he compensates by being with people, the six crore Gujaratis he claims to represent. He craves their affection, perhaps even their adulation, though he denies the weakness. After winning his first Assembly election in 2002, he said 'people do not sway me, I sway people'[1].

Campaigners must have excellent organizational skills. They are essentially mass mobilizers and animators. The Rashtriya Swayamsevak Sangh, (RSS) a Hindu nationalist outfit, taught Modi the alphabet of managing people and running an organization.

---

[1] S Prasannarajan, *India Today*, 6 January, 2003.

It gave him the knack of spotting people's capabilities, knitting them in teams, getting them to adopt ideas or tasks through group discussions, and motivating them to execute them efficiently. He acknowledges the debt to his biographer Nilanjan Mukhopadhyay[2].

The RSS has been an influence on Modi right from childhood. He began attending its *bal-shakhas* or morning drills at the age of eight. These consist of mild physical exercises, veneration of Bharat Mata (Mother India) and edifying nationalistic talk. In 1967, at age seventeen he joined college, but left home a year later reportedly vexed at his parents for bringing home the woman he was married to as a child. He went to the ashram of the Ramakrishna Mission in Rajkot, to its Belur Math in Kolkata and briefly spent some time with a reclusive sage in the Himalayas. For two years he thus wandered restlessly, apparently to discover himself. Upon returning to Ahmedabad he helped his uncle at his canteen at the state transport office becoming a canteen contractor himself. This is when he was introduced to RSS leaders.

They found him enthusiastic and strong-willed. Being from the caste of oil-pressers, they saw him as being able to draw youth from backward castes to an organization dominated by those higher up in the social heap. At their invite he moved into Hegdewar Bhawan, named after the founder of the RSS. Modi became an assistant to the *pracharaks* or propagandists and did household chores like sweeping and swabbing, and even the laundry of the founder of the Ahmedabad unit, a Maharashtrian Brahmin lawyer, known as Vakil Saheb. Modi stayed there till 1971.

Modi's subsequent vocation as an RSS propagandist developed his talent for oratory. This is a trait that he shares with many in the RSS and, its political wing, the Bharatiya Janata Party. Former Prime Minister Atal Behari Vajpayee was profound and witty. He could keep his audiences hanging on to his words — at times with

---

[2] *Narendra Modi, the Man, the Times,* Tranquebar, 2013

pauses so long their nails ached! Arun Jaitley, Sushma Swaraj and Uma Bharati can deliver verbal fusillades, as if they are reading from mental autocues. Former BJP President L K Advani is a study in enunciation. His successor M Venkaiah Naidu is known for laboured one-liners.

It can be said of Modi that he will suffocate if he does not communicate. The columnist Amulya Gopalakrishnan[3] says his 'voice is a tuned instrument that dips conspiratorially, thunders in defiance and shifts to a sincere, matter-of-fact tone when he is doing the successful CEO routine.' He answers a deep need, she says, because Manmohan Singh government's 'inability to visibly take charge or communicate its actions has created this yearning for confident leadership.'

For his detractors Modi's fascination for the microphone is an exercise in self-projection. Modi indeed is a compulsive publicist. There is nothing that he wants made known about this public life that is not out there hanging in the open. It is also a requirement that comes with the turf. 'It is a fair criticism that our top leaders have not communicated our achievements to the people,' Finance Minister P Chidambaram told the *Indian Express*[4] towards the end of the Congress-led United Progressive Alliance's second term in office. He gave the example of US President Barack Obama addressing the media twice or thrice a week, and British Prime Minister David Cameron being as regular.

On the dais, Modi is at once actor and spectator. His cadences and rhythm are hypnotic. He has incredible resonance with his admirers; they go into raptures when they hear him speak. And he loves grandstanding. There is much in his manner that is meant for show: the determined fist, the angry face, the sternly pointed index finger. He understands body language and can play to television

---

[3] *Indian Express 'Eye'*, 19-25 January, 2014.
[4] *Indian Express*, 20 January, 2014.

audiences. A former colleague[5] who was present at his rally at Dusshera maidan in Bhopal on 18 November 2013, said it had barely 5,000 people, or a tenth of the sport's venue's capacity but Modi was unfazed. Television audiences would not have known that it was thinly attended, because Modi pointed out to 'all you guys out there sitting on the balcony at the far end, can you hear me?' and the cameras recorded his gestures and speech, but not the non-existent persons 'on the balcony.' The deception would be amplified across the country because the organizers were doing the recording and providing the feed to television news networks.

Practice has perfected Modi's talent at mass mobilization. His apprenticeship began when the RSS gave him charge of the students' wing of the BJP in Gujarat. That was his initiation into student politics. His first encounter with mass protest happened during the 1974 Navnirman movement against the corrupt Congress government of Chimanbhai Patel.[6] It began with students of two government engineering colleges in Ahmedabad and Morvi protesting against the sudden increase in monthly hostel bills from Rs 80 to Rs 120. When the authorities refused to climb down, the students burnt down college property. Soon the protests rippled across the state as the entire student fraternity and trade unions joined in. The agitation against high food prices caused by inept handling of the drought that was scorching Gujarat became a rallying cry for Navnirman or reconstruction of society. Modi is said to have sat in on the fasts, but he may not have made much headway because students were wary of politicians initially, though they later invited freedom fighter Jayaprakash Narayan, who gave a

---

[5] Bhupedra Chaubey, National Affairs Editor of CNN-IBN. Also, 'Is Narendra Modi's Popularity on the Wane?' by Akash Deep Ashok, 21 November, 2013, *India Today* website. Accessed in February 2014.

[6] http://www.narendramodi.in/navnirman-movement-1974-when-student-power-rattled-the-unhealthy-status-quo/Acessed in February 2014.

call for *Sampoora Kranti* or Total Revolution against Indira Gandhi's government. Nevertheless, it brought him closer to them.[7]

During the Emergency, Modi worked to keep the RSS, which was banned, ventilating by organizing clandestine meetings, and supporting families of colleagues who were in prison. As Gujarat had a non-Congress government after the Navnirman movement, those opposed to the suspension of democracy made the state their refuge. Reports say that when a top RSS leader was arrested, Modi spirited away the next in command on his scooter. He got a female colleague to ferret out sensitive documents about the RSS's strategy from the arrested leader, while in police custody. Modi is said to have arranged the distribution of books and pamphlets on the denial of fundamental rights and the excesses of the Emergency.

When Indira Gandhi called an international conference of lawmakers of Commonwealth countries in Delhi, Modi arranged for books like *Indian Press Gagged, 20 Lies of Indira Gandhi* and *When Disobedience to Law is a Duty* smuggled to them. He was associated with an underground publication called *Muktwani*. Modi helped organize a meeting of opposition MPs in Gandhinagar. The Emergency brought him in touch with leaders like the socialist George Fernandes. While Modi's website conveys that he worked to undermine the undemocratic government at the centre, the lawyer and author A G Noorani writes that RSS leader Balasaheb Deoras was trying to get the ban on his organization lifted by writing 'cringing letters from prison' congratulating Indira Gandhi on her Independence Day speech and on a five-judge bench of the Supreme Court upholding the validity of her election on the basis of a retroactive amendment of the law that had disqualified her.[8]

---

[7] Achyut Yagnik and Shuchitra Sheth, *Ahmedabad: From Royal City to Mega City,* Penguin Books India, 2011.

[8] Excerpts from *Frontline,* 26 March, 1993, published in its 25th anniversary issue, January 2010, as Basic Instiuct by A G Noorani.

The RSS perhaps had adopted a forked strategy to survive those difficult days.

Upon his deputation to the BJP in 1987 and formal induction into politics, Modi played a behind-the-scenes role in organizing Nyaya Yatras to expose corruption in relief to the drought-affected people of Gujarat. Four such *yatras*, consisting of jeeps dressed up as chariots, toured 115 of the state's 182 talukas and 15,000 of Gujarat's 18,000 villages over forty days, says *India Today*. The *yatris* spoke to labourers, made them aware of their entitlements and checked work logs. 'Lakhs of rupees are being siphoned off daily by officials in the name of scarcity. The BJP is committed to exposing them,' Modi told the magazine's correspondent.[9]

Modi followed this up with the Lok Shakti Yatra, a three-month long affair covering about 10,000 villages. It began from the temple town of Ambaji and sought to project Keshubhai Patel as a leader of the entire state and not just of Saurashhtra. It was during this time that the RSS-affiliated Vishwa Hindu Parishad held its *Dharam Sansad* or religious parliament in Allahabad and announced a date for the *shilanyas* or ground-breaking ceremony for a grand Ram temple near the Babri Mosque in Ayodhya.

Festivals and processions integral to the practice of all religions in India have been used by the RSS and its subsidiaries for the political project of weaving Hindu society together by transcending divides of caste and tribe, using as hate objects those whose faith did not originate in India. In 1983, the Vishwa Hindu Parishad's Ekatmata Yatra tried to whip up fervour with three pilgrimages originating in Hardwar, Pashupatinath and Gangasagar. Holy water from these sacred sites was taken ceremoniously across the country to be poured into the sea at Rameshwaram, Kanyakumari and Somnath. Twenty-three smaller processions were part of this grand endeavour in Gujarat.

---

[9] Journey of Awareness, Statenotes, *India Today*, 15 January, 1988.

In 1987, the VHP organised the Ram-Janaki Dharma Yatra throughout Gujarat, including in tribal areas. Achuyut Yagnik and Shuchitra Sheth say in their book that as the cavalcade passed the town of Virpur at the junction of Kheda, Sabarkanta and Panchmahal districts, clashes broke out and for the first time tribals attacked Muslims.

The Ram Shila Puja Yatra was the massive event, when an estimated 275,000 consecrated bricks were brought from all over the country to the town of Ayodhya for the construction of a *'bhavya* (grand) Ram mandir' in 1989. Modi toured extensively in Gujarat exhorting participation and recruiting volunteers, many of whom were inducted into the BJP, raising its membership steeply.

Modi's day under the sun was 25 September, 1990, when BJP President L K Advani's Ram Rath Yatra set out from Somnath, the site of a temple that was first destroyed by Muslim invaders in 1026. For Advani, its rebuilding again and again was a symbol of *'lokshakti'* or people's power. Modi was given charge of the Gujarat leg and accompanied Advani till Mumbai. He had meticulously planned Advani's journey through 600 villages, with about fifty wayside rallies. Modi told Nilanjan Mukhopadhyaya that the *yatra* gave him an opportunity to 'develop my organizing ability.'

The use of *raths*[10] for political purposes was pioneered by Telugu movie star N T Rama Rao. After founding the Telugu Desam, NTR hit the road in a Chevrolet van converted into a 'Chariot of Awakening' and rode to victory in the 1983 assembly elections, on the platform of Telugu self-respect which had been badly dented by the Congress High Command's shabby treatment of Andhra chief minsters. The contraption, with rotating floodlights on both sides, and loudspeakers blaring songs of Telugu pride is said to have traversed 75,000 km. Advani's *rath* was an airconditioned

---

[10] http://www.hindu.com/2009/04/17/stories/2009041755071300.htm.

DCM Toyota mini-truck designed to look like Arjun's chariot in the television series *Mahabharata*. When Bihar Chief Minister Lalu Prasad, arrested Advani at Samastipur on October 23 and stopped its progress to Ayodhya, Modi called for a 'Week of Determination.' Denunciatory meetings were organised in 1,500 towns and villages of Gujarat;[11] and there were *bandhs* as well. Large-scale violence followed.

Modi got national display during the forty-seven-day Ekta Yatra of BJP president Murli Manohar Joshi that ended with the tricolour being hoisted at Lal Chowk in Srinagar. Modi was in element, doing a recce from Kanyakumari, charting out night halts, homing in on towns and cities with good connectivity so that maximum media mileage could be derived, and also keeping an eye for security threats. 'Modi led from the front,' says his website, conveying without false modesty that the charioteer was the star attraction. But as the convoy reached Kashmir, Joshi got nervous. The threat to life from Kashmiri separatists was palpable. Under cover of a security blanket, the flag was unfurled with about eighty *yatris* in attendance. The ceremony lasted less than fifteen minutes, says a RSS volunteer.[12] The *yatra* did little to flatter Joshi's image, but it gave Modi a worm's eye view of the nation.

Modi's latest mobilization of people is for a gigantic statue of Sardar Vallabhai Patel as a symbol of unity, in honour of India's first home minister who pieced together a country from a jumble of princely estates. The Sardar is the patron saint of Indian nationalism. In Gujarat others have claimed the mantle before. Chimanbhai modelled himself as Chhote Sardar. Former BJP President L K Advani, an MP from Gandhinagar, styled himself on the original Iron Man and called himself *'Loh Purush'* (despite being a rather

---

[11] Achyut Yagnik and Shuchitra Sheth in *The Shaping of Modern Gujarat*, Penguin Books India, 2005

[12] http://saswatpanigrahi.blogspot.in/2011/02/playing-nationalism-to-public-gallery.html (the guy is a self-confessed *swayamsevak*).

ineffective) home minister in Vajpayee's cabinet. For his followers, Modi is more muscular with a '56-inch wide chest.'

Mirroring the Ram Shila Pujan Yatra, pieces of iron from all over the country will be collected for the memorial at Sadhu Bet, an island three kilometres from the Sardar Sarovar dam across the Narmada. It is to be built by Turner Construction of the United States, in thirty-six months, at an estimated cost of Rs 2,500 cr. The boxes fitted with smart chips, will be supplied by the Sardar Patel Rashtriya Ekta Trust headed by Modi, and centrally tracked from Gujarat. Village level events where the contents will be dedicated to the nationalist cause will be monitored via satellite.

The Sangh Parivar is adept at invoking emotion to advance its causes. Modi, as the quintessential Sanghi, has projected himself as the custodian of Gujarati *asmita* or pride. The Sardar's imagery is meant to advertise Modi as a 'no-nonsense, business-like' leader in contrast to Manmohan Singh, whom Advani has called 'India's weakest Prime Minister.'

The BJP may not want a totem of unity almost double the height of the Statue of Liberty to be read as privileging nationalism over individual freedoms but the comparison is hard to resist. For Hindu nationalists devotion to the motherland is the supreme virtue. In an address to the Indian-American community in March, 2013, well before he was named the BJP's prime ministerial candidate, Modi said his slogan was, 'India First,' which for him meant that 'the country is above all religions and ideologies.'[13]

The formulation seems innocuous except that it is capable of menace. For the RSS and the BJP, the fact that Muslims and Christians have holy places outside India is proof of their extra-territorial loyalties. Sardar Patel has special appeal to the nationalists (though he banned the RSS after Mahatma Gandhi's assassination)

---

[13] 'India First,' is Modi's New Mantra, *The Hindu*, 11 March, 2013.

as he forced Muslim-majority Hyderabad and Kashmir to join the Indian union. Modi also indulges in smart wordplay. He told Reuters in an interview that since he was a Hindu and also a nationalist, he could be called a Hindu nationalist, though the phrase means more than the sum of the words constituting it.[14]

All totalitarian philosophies glorify the nation and the state. The Chinese Communist Party sees itself as the flag bearer of Chinese (meaning, Han) nationalism. It regards the suppression of liberties and sub-national assertions of identity like those of the Tibetans and Uighurs as necessary for national cohesion and the restoration of Chinese civilization to its past glory, when it saw itself at the centre of the universe. Development plus muscular nationalism is the formula for perpetuating one-party rule in China. Modi seeks to ride into South Block with development plus Congress Mukt Bharat.

The mobilization for the Statue of Unity also has Chinese echoes. (After initial fuss, little was heard of the project in the run up to the elections. Perhaps the BJP sensed that the campaign could be damaging. It is likely that it has been kept in abeyance for revival at an opportune moment.) In 1958 Mao Zedong launched the Great Leap Forward so that China 'walking on two legs' could be self sufficient in food through the collectivization of agriculture, and overtake the United States in manufacturing within a few years. Steel was the measure of industrial manhood. People were told to produce it in barnyard furnaces by melting pots, pans, rods and beams — anything that rusted. The historian Frank Dikotter says from 5.37 million tons in 1957, Mao set a target of 6.2 million tons to be met in February 1958, 8.5 million tonnes in May and 12 million tons in September. By end of 1960, China was to catch up with the Soviet Union and by 1962, overtake the United States with 100 million tons.[15] At the height of the steel fever, China

---

[14] Interview with BJP leader Narendra Modi, India Insight, Reuters 12 July, 2013.
[15] Frank Dikotter, *Mao's Great Famine*, Bloomsbury, 2010.

had about six lakh backyard furnaces. The landscape was stripped bare of trees to fire the smelters. Farming suffered as every ounce of manpower was diverted for steel production. Giganticism is an essential ingredient of national chauvinism. Often the consequences are terrible. The Great Leap landed China not on its feet but on its knees. The Statue of Unity can end up being its opposite if it promotes intolerance and preys on latent insecurities. Would not Mahatma Gandhi, or the Constitution as a freedom charter and symbol of the rule of law, been better choices?

But India First can also be a rallying cry for high national ambition, say of making India the third largest economy after United States and China by 2020.[16] Development can then indeed become a movement; unity of purpose welding the country together in joint endeavour. More evidence will be needed to pronounce that Modi can take everybody along, but he does not lack audacity and execution ability (These are dealt with in greater detail in a subsequent chapter.) Those inadequacies in our political leadership have weighed down India for a long time. As Raghav Bahl, a first-gen entrepreneur who crafted Delhi-based Network18 into a big television group says in his book:[17] 'There is only one risk for India, and that's the lack of confidence that India's own leaders have in its abilities and destiny. Every other disability stems from this endemic, ingrained complex that our policy makers suffer from. They peg India lower than an Indian can stretch to. They force India to punch below its weight. They are content being in the upper quartile, never quite believing that India has what it takes to be at the top, not just near the top.' The under-confidence of the political leadership and its corruption-induced stasis is complimented by a bureaucracy that

---

[16] India was 11th on UK consultancy, Cebr's annual World Economic League table, as published in *The Economic Times*, 27 December, 2013. Based on 2013 data, Cebr said India would be the third largest economy by 2028.

[17] Raghav Bahl, *Superpower? The Amazing Race Between China's Hare and India's Tortoise*, Portfolio, Penguin Books India, 2012.

is not only venal, but also compartmentalised in thinking. Turf wars inhibit administrative coherence and weaken governance.

To get his officials to march in unison to the drumbeat of development, and forge his government into a team Modi has deployed a couple of unique ideas. One of them is the annual thought camp or Chintan Shibir. Off-sites or retreats are commonly used by corporates to create bonding and team spirit. But it is an underutilised, even unused, device in government. Hasmukh Adhia, who was additional finance secretary, when I met him in 2014, said Modi had called a one-day annual meeting of district collectors and development officers in 2001 upon being nominated as chief minister. He saw ministers and secretaries exiting after delivering their lines and making presentations in half-hour slots. It was a revolving door. This is not how things should be done, Modi reasoned.

After winning his first election in 2002, Modi told his ministers and secretaries to make elaborate presentations. About one or two were held every week over three months from December to February. Each would last four to five hours till past 9 pm. Previously, departments would make a presentation to the chief secretary as a pre-Budget exercise. These would be a game of numbers. But now departments were told to supply activity reports, targets, budget outlays, the difficulties they foresaw both internally and externally and so on. It was a nuts and bolts operation. 'Besides benefiting him and the ministers, it was demystification, breaking the silos for us,' says a secretary. From this emerged the concept of the Chintan Shibirs.

Adhia, who was in charge of administrative reforms, had to translate the idea into practice. The first Chintan Shibir was held at Kevadia Colony near the picturesque Narmada dam in 2003. It was for two-and-a-half days. Ministers, all IAS officials from secretaries to collectors and district development officers, the top police official and the principal forest conservator — about 250 of them — attended. The aim was to make governance less formal, reduce distance between the top and bottom rungs, and create informal networks, which officials could leverage to get things done. Anyone could sit anywhere for meals, including with the Chief Minister; the rule was that queues could not be broken.

Chintan Shibir days are long. They begin early in the morning with yoga exercises and end with dinner at 8 pm. Cultural events follow; they are meant for talent display. The structure has improved over the years. The chief secretary now holds pre-camp meetings to distil six themes for discussion. The discussants are assigned at random without regard to their current portfolios so that fresh thinking is brought to bear on an issue. Several district level initiatives have been applied state-wide, Bhagyesh Jha's one-day governance, or same-day provision of citizen services being one of them.

The inspiration for one-day governance was Irfan Pathan's match-winning bowling performance against Pakistan in 2004. 'The entire nation is proud of him,' Modi told his Baroda-based father over the phone as India won the revival series. Bhagyesh Jha, collector of the district, recalls visiting Pathan's home. On the way back, he asked the accompanying police commissioner, 'how do we bring one-day cricket to governance?' It was not a rhetorical question. Jha got his colleagues to give serious thought to it. They decided on one-day governance, where the people of Baroda, arrayed on one side, would bowl applications, and officials would bat back the requested services by the end of the match. Jha says an analysis showed that there were seventy-two instances of citizen interface with the government at the district level for services like birth, caste, income and domicile certificates. Six of these could be electronically given within a day if applicants provided the information that was asked for. This is how the first Nagarik Seva Kendra (citizen service centre) was set up in Baroda. After being discussed at a Chintan Shibir, it was applied across the state as Jan Seva Kendras.

Jan Seva Kendras today deal with 156 kinds of public services. Of these a fifth, like land records, alterations in ration cards and land revenue payments, are processed within two hours. Half of the rest are delivered the same day, and the other half can take between three to ninety days. Certificates that would take days to process and blobs of speed money, like land records, can now be obtained within no time and on payment of a nominal fee. This has been facilitated by e-Dhara or the computerization of 1.5 million land records, an idea that emerged from the first thought camp.

Modi and his acolytes like to project that whatever is good in governance was conceived by their icon. Modi himself seems to believe that he has an inborn capacity for offbeat ideas. Whatever the veracity of that belief, Modi certainly is a good learner. 'He has the ability to convert ignorance into bliss, adversity into opportunity,' says an IIT-educated secretary. 'You sound like a starry-eyed disciple,' I tease him. 'Too old for that,' he retorts. Contrary to the impression that he is a self-opinionated, pompous and dismissive dictator who loves listening to his own voice, Modi is open to ideas, says a newly retired bureaucrat, who maintains that he has never shied from making his views known within, of course, tacitly understood red lines. 'Modi on the dais is quite different from Modi in administration,' is the opinion of an Ahmedabad Urban Development Authority official.

To convey the message that constraints can be overcome with smart thinking, Modi gives the example of S R Rao, who was commissioner of Surat Municipal Corporation when it was ravaged by bubonic plague in 1994. The epidemic killed fifty-two people and forced 300,000 migrant workers to flee the diamond polishing and textile hub. There was panic across the country, expressed in people walking about with surgical masks on. The antibiotic tetracycline vanished from pharmacies, foreign travellers avoided India and restrictions on cargo movement affected international trade. The World Health Organization estimated India's loss at $1.7 billion. Rao put adversity to good use and cleaned up Surat, by instituting a series of measures like desilting the river Tapti, de-clogging the drains, expediting waste management projects, and empowering the sanitation staff. If Surat could do it, Modi said, what was holding back the other municipal corporations?

Examples of excellence in administration from other states are appreciated in the camps and their practitioners are invited to speak. Nagaland's chief secretary R S Pandey was the invitee in 2008. He had involved Naga village communities to share management responsibility for schools, health centres, water supply and rural roads building on the unique social capital available in the state. This 'communitization' approach was commended by the United Nations and won Pandey the Prime Minister's award for administrative excellence. Pandey, who was petroleum secretary and the centre's interlocutor with the Nagas, is now a Modi *bhakt*. Upon joining the BJP a few months before the 2014 Lok Sabha elections he had this to say about Modi: 'I clearly remember my first meeting with him. He invited me to the Chintan Shibir about five years ago....He was the only CM who was interested in understanding the new delivery model. His mission is to keep innovating and keep improving, unlike many departments in the center, which are gripped by inaction or policy paralysis.'[18]

There was resistance to the retreats when they were initiated. Officials thought nothing good would come out of them. But the opposition has wilted. A getaway from capital Gandhinagar helps participants focus their minds. Motivation mavens are invited and management games are played. Among the invitees was a monk from

---

[18] http://articles.economictimes.indiatimes.com/2013-12-14/news/45191138_1_policy-paralysis-tough-action-entire-country.

Delhi's Akshardham temple. He spoke on work-flow management at the Rs 200 cr project which rivals Mughal monuments in scale.

A problem-solving attitude is desired mental mode at the camps. 'We do not discuss what is bad, what is lagging. When we are talking about the good naturally we can eliminate the bad things. This is the way of working,' Modi said in an interview. Vexatious issues that have large inter-departmental footprints like tribal welfare or universal schooling have a greater chance of getting resolved through consensus when released from the confines of their silos. Modi has instructed that decisions taken at the camps should become government orders immediately upon the return of officials to Gandhinagar without having to go through another approval drill.

But intent does get lost in the translation. To give a flavour, the minutes of the camp held at Shanku's water park in Mehsana in February 2011 had a suggestion for review of action on decisions taken at the previous event, and a discussion on the reasons for inaction. While there was top-notch analysis of problems, the emphasis should be to finding solutions, the minutes said, though one would have expected the one to lead to the other. Administrative hurdles get blurred because of the focus on development, was another complaint. Issues of law and order, tax administration, infrastructure and project evaluation are not taken up at the Chintan Shibirs but should be as these tend to bog down district officials. Despite seven camps being held, departments were still not talking to each other as they should, the minutes said. The eighteen examples of best practices on which presentation were made at Shanku's park covered familiar territory: garbage management, use of technology in recruitments, provision of certificates and approvals online, grievance redress, rain water conservation, provision of housing to nomadic tribals and the like, indicating that even in one of the best governed states, the administrative apparatus that touches people is yet to come to grips with basic issues. There were gripes that the three-days were densely packed; there was not enough time for informal interaction in the evenings and the presentations could be crisper. But the Shibir as a concept scored high marks and a suggestion was made for patenting the format!

At the 2004 retreat an official recalls Modi saying something like this: 'You do a lot of work for the government. You do it because you are told. It is your duty. Why don't you do something which is beyond your remit, for your own satisfaction and for the public good, using the flexibility that you have in use of funds? Do something that is dear to your heart.' He named the initiative Swantha Sukhay. (It had another not-so-tangential benefit. The ambition of an official's Swantha Sukhay project gave the chief minister a measure of their motivation.)

Organisations are only as good as the people comprising them. But their talent and competence can go to waste if they feel helpless or find their work unexciting. Everyone seeks job satisfaction, but it eludes most of us. Most jobs are far from satisfying but they have to be satisfied; there is no escaping the grind. But the sparkle of inner joy can flatter humdrum existence. That Swantha Sukhay gave vent to a pent up need to do good was obvious from the response. In the first two years, 256 projects were initiated, of which forty-five were chosen for commendation. One of them was the kitchen gardens attached to Baroda *anganwadis*.

A quarter of Baroda's population was tribal when this project was initiated. Gujaratis are predominantly vegetarian, but tribals were not in the habit of eating green leafy vegetables. For lack of iron, expectant mothers and kids tended to be anaemic. Baroda's chief medical officer found 94 percent of surveyed mothers to be moderately or mildly anaemic, when I did a television series on governance on CNBC-TV18. Why not supplement their diet with veggies grown on *anganwadi* plots, thought M Thennarasan, a 2000 batch IAS officer from Thanjavur in Tamil Nadu, who was posted as development officer in the district. The idea needed some convincing, but the three agencies involved came around with some persuasion.

An audit done by the Sardar Patel Institute for Public Administration found that 20,000 children had benefited. Their haemoglobin levels had risen by 0.6 grams/dl each. Those covered by the programme were cured of Vitamin A deficiency as well.

Thennarasan's successor R J Patel called the gardens green blood banks and prevailed upon government doctors to distribute seeds to tribals along with medicines, so that they would be convinced of the health benefits. When I met him he was collector of Basakantha district. The day was Ramnavami and Ambedkar Jayanti rolled in one. Though a holiday, Patel had called officials to take an eight-point pledge to serve *dalits*, tribals, destitutes and the disabled. A bit of an eccentric, I was told that his obsession with public work had alienated him from his family! A cassette of songs he had composed during his previous posting extolled the virtues of eating vegetables. He had summoned Lord Krishna for advocacy.

In Ahmedabad, a Swantha Sukhay initiative was also a test of the Chief Minister's faith in his officials. The road transport officer wanted to get the city's smoke-belching autorickshaws converted to compressed gas. The traffic police chief and the collector were supportive, as pollution in Ahmedabad brought tears to eyes. There were 35,000 offending vehicles, but municipal elections were at hand and votes were at risk. On an assurance by the officials that the conversion would be done well before the polls — and without a hitch, the chief minister gave the green signal.

Resistance from vehicle owners withered as loans were arranged. The manufacturer Bajaj Auto, pitched in with a concession. Gas distributors gave free fuel vouchers. These palliatives resulted in 22,200 autos switching over to compressed gas, and 12,000 new autos plying. Over five million Ahmedabadis could breathe easy.

The measures to save rain water in the arid tribal district of Dahod are another example of a small step with a big impact. The district not only gets little rain, whatever it gets is not retained; such is the quality of the soil. The project cost nearly Rs 4 cr. It was initiated by the district's rural development agency. The twenty-eight check dams, 3,700 *bori* or sand-bagged *bunds*, 4,500 farm ponds and five lift irrigation schemes did not convert the district into an oasis, but it made summers less punishing.

Political leaders have to face voters every five years, if not earlier. Those who are in politics for the long term, and do not see it as just an investment with the quickest returns dread administrative apathy. Pravin K Lahiri, who retired as chief secretary in 2005 recalls Chief Minister Madhavsinh Solani joking about the dinosaur which took two months to react when bitten. 'Modi believes in campaigns,' says Lahiri. 'They give focus to the administration. Otherwise inertia sets in.'

In the first decades of Communist Party rule in China mass campaigns were a feature of daily life. The drives publicised new policies and tried to engender compliance. The purpose was to ensure that the goals of the party were internalized and to get people to 'emancipate themselves step by step.'[19]

The fear of revolutionary fervour flagging and challengers undercutting his power kept Mao and the party on edge. The Hundred Flowers Campaign encouraged dissent but was meant to smoke out the critics, who were purged in the Anti-Rightist campaign that followed. The challenge to Mao's authority following the starvation deaths of thirty to forty million people during the Great Leap Forward resulted in the decade long Cultural Revolution, where colleges were closed down and elites were sent to villages to learn from the masses.

---

[19] Jeffrey N Wasserstrom, *China in the 21st Century: What Everyone Needs to Know*, Oxford University Press, 2010.

As the Indian context is different, an exact corollary cannot be drawn, but mobilizing the administration for agricultural extension work, saving the girl child, ensuring universal enrolment, improving quality of schooling, investing in child health, making the state litter-free, conserving rain water and the chief minister himself addressing complaints by videoconference on the last Thursday of every month, are meant to bring officials in contact with people so that policies are not divorced from reality, while also shoring up Modi's popularity with people and grip on the party.

Agriculture has been the real surprise in Gujarat's development story. This semi-arid state has clocked 8 percent average farm growth in the past decade, while in the country as a whole the sector has moved to the rhythm of a chant (3.1 percent). Among the various reasons cited by professors Ravindra Dholakia and Samar Datta of the Indian Institute of Management, Ahmedabad, the rejuvenation of the agricultural extension apparatus is very important.

India's former Chief Economic Adviser Shankar Acharya says[20] agricultural extension system established in the two decades after independence has 'suffered serious entropy and decay' across the country. In Gujarat, he says, 'a systematic and massive renewal of agricultural extension systems was carried out under the Krishi Mahotsav programme,' which began in 2005. About one lakh officials from eighteen departments visit farmers in their villages for a month before the onset of monsoons. They test the soil, prescribe nutrients that must be replenished, recommend crops to be grown, suggest hybrid seeds to be used, and give advice on profitable cultivation. Planning has descended from rarefied offices and labs to the block and village levels. Krishi Mahotsavs are a celebration in agricultural outreach.

Gujarat has realised that agriculture is no longer a subsistence activity and must be conducted like a business operation. Farming

---

[20] Shankar Acharya, Agriculture: Be Like Gujarat, *Business Standard,* 14 July, 2014.

is akin to an industrial process, where plants are factories to be managed scientifically. The annual Krishi Mahotsav is an exercise in mindset change and brings the administration closer to people.

The same philosophy informs the girl-child school enrolment drives called Kanya Kelavani and Shala Praveshotsav. Every year officials have to visit five villages on each of three days. That is fifteen villages and fifteen speeches per official to urge the point that a girl taught is a family educated. They have to visit the homes of children who have dropped out, convince their parents why they cannot be out of school, and personally escort them to school for re-enrolment. This has been going on for seven years. In the process, officials realize that education is a state priority and it should get cross-department support.

Now that near one hundred percent enrolment has been achieved, the emphasis is on improving the quality of schooling. Under the Gunotsav (Quality Festival) drive, every official (and not just from the education department) is required to visit three villages over three days. That is about 3,000 officials vetting 9,000 schools. They begin by attending the prayer meeting in the morning assembly, watching the yoga display and observing teacher-children interaction. This is followed by class visits and testing of students for English, Gujarati and math skills.

All this may sound good on paper but in reality officials may not be fervent. They might just go through the motions. But one cannot quibble about the intention behind the drive. Of course, there is a risk that schools will suffer for no fault of theirs. The inspectors may be whimsical, erratic or indifferent. Factoring this, the assessment system is being reset to minimize, and even eliminate, subjectivity.

An example of hype not matching reality is Nirmal Gujarat, a drive initiated in 2007 to make Gujarat clean and sanitary through management of garbage, treatment of effluents, air pollution control and a mass toilet installation drive. But after a week-long tour of Gujarat by state transport buses in 2012 a memory that endured in me was that of extensive litter and filth. Dwarka was a shock (unlike Somnath which was well-kept). No municipal broom seemed to have touched it; the *ghats* on the river banks were swamped with garbage. How could this happen to a pilgrimage centre in a state that champions Hindutva? Sudhir Mankad, a former chief secretary says Nirmal Gujarat should have been of five years duration to achieve its objectives.

'Modi believes that officials want to do good,' says Adhia. Gujarat officials are allowed long tenures, at times so long they get tired of it. Adhia was education secretary from 2001 to 2013! His two predecessors served four-year stints each. Anand Mohan Tiwari was tribal affairs secretary for 5.5 years despite a vigorous campaign against him by various special interest groups. Modi apparently believes that transferring an incompetent official only shifts their incompetence elsewhere. It does not improve their abilities.

Modi does not let anyone interfere in postings and transfers. He can do this because MLAs and MPs are beholden to him; it is he who wins them elections. Alexander K Luke, an IIT-educated officer, who was known for his managerial acumen says his transfer from the profitable Gujarat Minerals Development Corporation to the troubled Gujarat State Fertiliser Corporation happened within a week, at his request. The shifting of the corruption-prone drip irrigation scheme from the agriculture department to the specially created Gujarat Green Revolution Company, a subsidiary of the Bharuch-based Gujarat State Fertilizer Corporation, of which Luke was chairman, also happened with little fuss. There was no way that the agriculture minister could object.[21]

Modi may not have put professional managers in charge of state enterprises but he has professionalized their management by

---

[21] Conversation with A K Luke, 24 February, 2014.

posting able bureaucrats, unlike many other states where politicians preside and aggrandize themselves.

The approach has worked. Audit reports say that when Modi took over there were forty state-owned companies and statutory corporations, including the electricity utility, which was later broken up and corporatized. They earned a return of 3.33 percent on employed capital of Rs 15,000 cr. The latest report says forty-one state-owned companies made a profit of nearly Rs 9,000 cr giving a return of around 7 percent on employed capital; ten companies made losses of Rs 400 cr in all.

Speaking to chartered accountants in Delhi at end of February 2014, Modi said no sooner was he named as chief minister in 2001, than delegations came to him, though he was yet to be sworn in. One of them was of GSFC workers. The company was making losses, the workers feared for their jobs and they beseeched him for the sake of their families. Modi sought some time to think over, as he was new to matters administrative. His officials said the choice was binary: loss making state enterprises were closed down or sold off. Modi settled on a third alternative: that of reviving them.

Luke was the officer chosen. He practices agriculture in Kerala, where he retired to after resigning from the IAS when he got a transfer order. It was a promotion as additional chief secretary (transport), but for Luke it was a humiliation. He was expecting to be celebrated; Modi would not indulge him.

Luke had done a great job at GSFC. When he had taken over in May 2003, the company was bleeding. The loss for the previous year was Rs 383 cr. The stock price was Rs 17 according to the Bombay Stock Exchange. It had sought legal protection from creditors. The Reserve Bank had agreed to its bank debt being restructured. Luke had turned it around by following his philosophy of 'ethical management'. His website, www.ethicalmanagementluke.com elaborates this as doing whatever is good for an organization. It is not a call to piety. 'I was a person of average intrinsic ability,' Luke says. 'Ethically armed, I won luminous victories.' Luke believes that 'ethicals' like him, that is, persons with even ordinary ability but steadfast commitment can move mountains.

Luke had previously made Gujarat Alkalies profitable, and got the juices flowing at Sardar Sarovar Nigam. At GSFC he got all the plants working to capacity. He entered into a joint venture to produce phosphoric acid, a fertilizer ingredient, in Tunisia. There was no retrenchment of workers or cash support from the government. By the time he quit in November 2006, the stock price was Rs 185. In between, it had closed at a high of Rs 243. The company had turned profitable; it had prematurely retired a ten year loan. Modi was appreciative but displeased.

The reason: Luke had vetoed a proposal to make a higher-than-usual contribution to the chief minster's relief fund, and had resisted the transfer of an employee, who was not financially corrupt. He was also charged with showing disrespect to elected representatives. (Luke's colleagues said he used to be blunt and in your face.) Luke's defence: 'I hold that reviving organizations under me was an expression of the highest respect to the elected representative.'

This is more than Modi will tolerate. He will not let anybody defy or outshine him, qualities that Luke cannot agree with: 'Modi does not forget, he does not forgive and he does not reward,' he asserts.

The last is applicable for those not pliant. If they are, capable officials are rewarded with long tenures and post-retirement sinecures. Step out of line and the first two bits of Luke's equation come into play.

Manoj Mitta's book presents some nuggets of evidence[22]. Rahul Sharma, as Bhavnagar district's superintendent of police in 2002,

---

[22] Manoj Mitta, *The Fiction of Fact-Finding*, HarperCollins Publishers India, 2014.

had ordered his men to fire on rioters thus denying the partisans among them an excuse for inaction. Twice a mob tried to set fire to a madrasa housing 400 students but prompt police action thwarted them. For his professionalism, Sharma was transferred within twenty-four hours to Ahmedabad's control room as deputy commissioner of police — an off field job. (Modi held the home portfolio.) Fortunately, Sharma's posting turned out to be a blow for justice. Being an engineer (from IIT Kanpur) and a law graduate, he realized that cell phone call data records would mark the movements of rioters and their leaders. He collected the data and gave the CD to an inquiry commission. This is how minister Maya Kodnani was nailed in two cases of rioting for which she got the death penalty. But for blowing the whistle without permission, disciplinary action was initiated against Sharma. He was charged with four counts of indiscipline.

Modi has a comprehensive — and rather unnerving — grip on the administration. He puts police and the official intelligence gathering machinery to good use. Even private citizens are snooped on. This was revealed when G L Singhal, a police officer accused in the Ishrat Jahan fake encounter case was arrested and put in jail. After his teenage son committed suicide, Singhal decided to bare all. He handed over a bunch of recorded phone conversations to the Central Bureau of Investigation including those with former home minister Amit Shah about tabs on a female architect on behalf of 'Saheb'. Those acquainted with Modi also say that he has an informal grapevine, developed over long years in public life.

But he has another explicit way of keeping tabs on the administration. On the last Thursday of every month, Modi takes up people's grievances that arrive at him through a three-tier filtration process. Complaints are categorized as first-time, long-pending and policy matters and, if they defy resolution at lower levels, are put up to Modi. The chief minister, senior officials and the complainant are linked through a state-wide videoconferencing system. This is called

Swagat, a neat acronym for the state wide attention on grievances by application of technology. It was instituted in 2003 and has won an UN award for transparency, accountability and responsiveness. It relies on a state-wide computer network that connects all ministries and departments, district headquarters and taluka offices. Since 2011, it has gone rural, to villages.

Andhra chief minister Chandrababu Naidu would use videoconferencing to simultaneously address district collectors on a regular basis, or consult cabinet ministers on various issues like the electric power situation in the districts, *rythu* (farmer) bazaars, commodity prices, implementation of road works, public health situation and law and order.

Then there are district level initiatives like Lokvani, an Internet-based grievance redress system which collector Amod Kumar installed in Sitapur district in 2004. In a large country like India 'good governance is not possible with e-governance,' Kumar said when I met him a few years later for a television series. Lokvani and Kumar were awarded the Prime Minister's award for excellence in public administration. As UP's special secretary for information technology, Zohra Chatterji bought the software from the non-profit society which Kumar had set up and gave it to all the other sixty-nine (one less than now) districts of the state. In 2009, Nikhil Dey co-founder of the Mazdoor Kisan Shakti Sanghatan persuaded collector Manju Rajpal to install Lokvani in Rajasthan's Bhilwara district. Lokvani has fallen into disuse in UP with neither chief minister Mayawati nor her successors warming up to it.

But few chief ministers make use of technology to make their administrations responsive. Quite a few of them rely on *janata durbars* or mass drives. Modi is quite an exception.

Modi runs a clean administration, so goes the lore. He is single, and he keeps his family at a distance, having left home at a young age. So he is not personally corrupt. But talk to any resident and they will say that the administration is not free of corruption. Little happens without palm grease. The use of technology to provide public services has reduced the size of bribes, but has not eliminated petty corruption. Boot-legging in a state under Prohibition generates huge amount of black money. In some places, it is so blatant that liquor is sold in the vicinity of police posts. A Delhi-based corporate executive, and a long-time observer of the state says three forms of corruption are prevalent in Gujarat: *shukrana* (Urdu for thank you in kind), *nazrana* (a tribute, say at the time of Diwali), and *mehentana* (payment for services rendered) but not *jabrana* (extortion).

And Modi need campaign finance. His Prime Ministerial challenge, begun a year ahead of the polls, has soaked up a tremendous amount of money. Modi relies on a few corporate favourites to keep his politics whirring. It is possible to see it as preferable to spreading the 'levy' over the entire industry. So how are favours returned? A spokesperson for one of the capitalist 'cronies' says they are obliged through tailored policies or grants of land. Gujarat has the second largest swathe of waste land after Rajasthan in districts like Kutch, Surendranagar and Panchmahals which the government can give away cheaply.[23] Civil society groups decry this as alienation of village commons or pastures. But officials and corporate leaders assert that better value is created when it is put to industrial or infrastructural use. Care is taken not to acquire fertile agricultural land. Even when it becomes necessary to do so, coercion is rarely resorted to. Labanyendu Mansingh, an official who held various positions including that of principal secretary, industries and retired from the central government as secretary, consumer affairs, says the practice is for the revenue department or the Gujarat Industrial Development Corporation to pass a notification under the land acquisition law as soon as an investor

---

[23] Pravin K Laheri, in conversation on 27 February, 2014.

homes in on a factory site. This bars further land sales. Speculators are kept out and land prices are frozen. The investor then negotiates the price with land owners. The brokers usually are retired revenue officers. They enter into sale agreements and on that basis the government passes a consent decree.

This is a reason why farmer unrest has been the exception in Gujarat unlike in West Bengal, Maharashtra or Orissa. But there are examples of public anger boiling over as in Bhavnagar district over the location of a cement plant and in Mehsana over the acquisition of farm land for a special investment region. (Yet despite farmers of Sanand making good money from sale of land to Tata Motors for its small car factory, the BJP lost this newly-carved assembly seat, considered to be its stronghold, by a narrow margin, reportedly due to rebellion in its ranks.)

Modi is focused. He gives a lot of time to his job. 'Very few will give the number of hours that he does,' says Laheri. Modi excels in execution. Anil Das, a consultant with the Asian Development Bank says, 'Modi wanted every child to know the basics of earthquake resistant construction,' after the devastating Kutch trembler of 2001. The initial policy decisions were taken by chief minister Keshubhai Patel, but upon stepping into Patel's shoes later that year, Modi ensured that the administration delivered.

ADB was one of the financing agencies. Modi insisted that all reconstructed houses should be earthquake resistant. A massive awareness campaign was launched There were 'shake table tests' in villages to demonstrate the difference between earthquake-resistant techniques and traditional methods. No building plan was passed without vetting. Material and houses were randomly tested. Competent officials were put in charge. The boundaries of Bhuj, the district headquarters, were extended and the city rebuilt in a planned manner. People were persuaded to give up land for wider roads; many were relocated from crowded clusters.

Kutch's economic reconstruction is a story of intelligent design. To attract industry, the state threw in tax concessions, interest subsidies and infrastructures. With its vast, sparely populated land, reserves of minerals, port connectivity and Narmada water supply, this arid district was transformed.

While life in the RSS has given Modi some stiff ideas, he can be flexible. There is no evidence, though, that this extends to core, Hindutva, beliefs. Modi has changed his stance on education; he has done the most to promote the use of English so as not to impair the career prospects of students while maintaining that learning happens best in one's mother tongue. Similarly, while being a votary of privatization, Modi has refrained from privatizing the state electricity utilities for fear that private entities will neglect customers with poor paying capacity. His position on globalization differs from the RSS stance on *swadeshi*. And he is quick to take decisions. Satyam Computer's disgraced founder, Ramalinga Raju's Emergency Management and Research Institute (EMRI) was given approval for running an emergency ambulance service in Gujarat after a short but detailed presentation. Modi is an effective campaigner and mobilizer because he is himself charged up. His governance is efficient because his administration is cohesive and he leads from the front. It has done a lot of good not only on the economic front but also in social sectors like education. Healthcare achievements do not speak well for a developed state, though efforts have not been wanting. Many of his initiatives and innovations can be applied nationally, with profit.

But there is a democracy deficit. Modi is no respecter of checks and balances. Unlike leaders of Western democracies who allow themselves to be questioned by the media at all times, he seldom addresses press conferences or subjects himself to journalistic scrutiny. He has also not reached out in sincerity to the Muslim community. Modi's governance is good in parts.

2. The Shield of Development

Investment promotion has been the leitmotif of all Gujarat administrations since it became a state in 1960, but Modi leads visibly — and loudly — from the front. Development is Modi's best advertising and defence.

The impression one gets from his speeches, blogs and fans is that Modi stands at the cusp of Gujarat's economic history. His hagiographers divide Gujarat's business history into AM or Ante-Modi and PM or Post Modi. But the state's chief ministers regardless of party affiliation have consistently given a thrust to industrial development. There is a Gujarat model of development which Modi has tailored to his style. The unrelenting media scrutiny of Modi following the riots that happened under this watch perhaps forced him to dwell on the economy more than he otherwise would. It was a political compulsion and a personal necessity.

Bihar politician Lalu Yadav offers a parallel example. Having acquired a reputation as wrecker-in-chief of the state's sliding economy through three terms as chief minister, in person and by proxy, Lalu used his five-year stint as union railway minister between 2004 and 2009 for an image makeover. By putting in charge an able official to reform the railways and by providing him political cover, Lalu was able to substantially improve railway finances. Freight rates went up, especially of export cargo that could bear a higher tariff, passenger fares were raised on the sly and carrying capacity was increased by running faster, longer and heavier trains. Lalu was invited to speak to management students in India and abroad about how he 'milked the cow'. He was hailed as a turnaround artiste. A book on the theme was also published by Oxford University Press.

While the iconography of Gujarat's development is jazzed up, it is not a mask. Modi invites skepticism because of the publicity overkill. He likes to project a larger than life image. So do his fans who regard him as the mascot of Hindutva and the embodiment of virile Hindu nationhood. For votaries of market economics, associating Modi with development is a way of glossing over his illiberal streak.

The RSS, which schooled Modi for public life, understands that successful political communication depends on assertion, reiteration and amplification. It knows that words and phrases can be infused with the meaning it intends through constant forceful repetition by an array of voices over a period of time. Thus the equal treatment of religious communities becomes 'pseudo-secularism'. (The term finds resonance because of the 'opportunistic communalism' of the parties that are not ideologically communal.) Constitutional privileges for minorities to help preserve their distinct identity and even uplift their disadvantaged through affirmative action is termed 'appeasement' or 'vote bank politics' (but majority communalism is not). The Babri Masjid morphs into a 'disputed structure', the celebration of diversity is a threat to unity, when Hindu girls fall for Muslim boys it is 'love jehad,' Muslim radicals are 'terrorists' but when Hindu vigilantes indulge in violence it is a 'spontaneous reaction'.

Modi has a sound claim to the title of Vikas Purush. Since the beginning of the past decade which is almost co-terminus with Modi's career as Chief Minister, Gujarat has grown at an average annual clip of 8.85 percent. This is the highest among major states and one and a half percentage points faster than the growth rate of all states combined. Uttarakhand has done much better[1] but it is a much smaller state, with population a sixth of Gujarat's. Haryana is at par in pace of growth, while Maharashtra is one step behind. Both the states out-do Gujarat in per capita GDP. Bihar chief minister Nitish Kumar claims his growth model is better as it is 'inclusive'. True, the state has grown at 8 percent over the past decade but economic bounce is easier at lower levels of GDP; the Bihari's slice of the economic cake is one quarter the size of the Gujarati's.

Those who abhor Modi's Hindutva politics grudge him credit. They say that enterprise is ingrained in the Gujarati DNA. 'I will accept his claims to development, if he can repeat his performance in Bihar,' says a former (Muslim) deputy collector of Gandhinagar. Gujarat's economy has been built by its business-friendly bureaucracy, says a (secular) Gujarati editor of a news portal. Even Modi's supporters claim the state's entrepreneurial energy will find expression even without a helpful government. Gujarat's economy will be on multi-pilot, not just autopilot, says a Hindutva-spouting journalist. Leftists belittle Modi's 'neo-liberal' achievements as benefiting capitalist cronies and big companies while doing little to alleviate poverty. Far from being in the service of five crore Gujaratis, Modi is at the service of five *crorepatis*, says the Opposition. His economic policies are for Dani, Adani and Nathwani, is another variant of this theme. Gujarat's underperformance on social measures also opens up a flank for attack.

∽

Being at the intersection of the Spice and Silk Routes, and with a coastline about a quarter of India's, Gujarat has indeed been an

---

[1] Uttarakhand's growth between during 2000-12 was 11.68 percent, that of Gujarat 8.85 percent and Haryana's 8.84 percent. Maharshtra grew at 8.09 percent and Tamil Nadu at 7.97 percent, a tad higher than Bihar's 7.96 percent. *Source:* Planning Commission.

incubator of enterprise. Trade and commerce infuses the Gujarati worldview. It is also the lens through which the world views them. *Bania*, the generic term for traders, is said to be a Portuguese corruption of Vaniya, Gujarat's main merchant caste. Business has influenced its choice of religion: Jainism, and Vaishnavism, an especially pacific strand of Hinduism. Even those who converted to Islam — the Bohras, the Memons and Khojas — perhaps had ease of doing business in mind, as Islam has no injunction against crossing the seas. The scent of trade led them to Africa and with economic heft they, over time, secured political clout there.

Surat was India's principal port. This is where the English East India Company opened a beachhead in 1608. The British came there as traders, but started their colonial conquest a century and a half later from the east, through Bengal. They created conditions for industrial capitalism. Bengalis and Parsis were the first Indians to set up industries. Ahmedabad-based business historian Dwiendra Tripathi tells me that trading, which yielded quick and high returns, initially suppressed the Gujarati instinct for industrial risk and innovation. But they soon caught up. The share of manufacturing (excluding mining, quarrying, and utilities like electricity and water) in Gujarat's economy is 24 percent, compared to India's 16 percent.

But enterprising people need enabling conditions. To say the economy can propel itself autonomously is to deny the leavening role of government and leadership. Management professor Ravindra Dholakia says Gujarat underperformed the nation in the 1980s.[2] Annual growth averaged 4.1 percent, slower than the nation's 5.2 percent. Private enterprise-suppressing central policies may have

---

[2] Regional sources of growth acceleration in India, IIMA, March 2009. At constant 1993-94 prices Gujarat grew at 4.16 percent between 1980-81 and 1991-92 while India grew at 5.29 percent. Between 1991-92 and 2003-04, the respective rates were 6.61 percent and 5.91 percent.
http://www.iimahd.ernet.in/assets/snippets/workingpaperpdf/2009-03-06Dholakia.pdf.

directed the state's vitality into the informal sector, he said in a conversation. But a diversified economy, commercialized agriculture and relatively high degree of urbanization brought the state into the economic frontline, when reforms were ushered in.

It is true that Gujarat has a large share of capital-intensive industries. It ranks first in fixed capital with 16 percent of the country's share. Being endowed with oil and gas, Gujarat is the natural location of the refining and petrochemical industries. It has also used its long coastline to turn deprivation to advantage. Despite lacking iron ore, Gujarat has the single largest flat steel plant at Hazira.[3] Distance from domestic coal mines and the inefficiency of the Indian railways, has spurred port-based power plants that use imported coal. Tax concessions given after the 2001 earthquake, and a large private port, have made arid Kutch the global hub for pipeline manufacture[4] and the second fastest growing district, population-wise, after Surat, according to the last census. Salt reserves have brought the heavy chemical (like caustic soda and soda ash) industry to the state. It is the leading producer of drugs, along with Andhra Pradesh. The Ahmedabad belt has become the latest hub of automobile manufacture, after the Delhi, Pune and Chennai regions. The small car Nano has done little to improve the fortunes of Tata Motors, but Sanand, where the factory is located, has attracted other car makers like Ford, and auto component manufacturers too. Maheshwar Sahu, who retired as industries secretary at the end of January 2014, says investment worth Rs 70,000 cr could flow-in within five years.[5]

---

[3] Essar Steel at Hazira, which uses steel pellets produced at the Vizag, and transported by sea.
[4] Anjar: New Global Pipeline Hub, Swaminathan Anklesaria Aiyar, *Times of India*, 3 August, 2008. Also, my conversation with officials of Jindal Saw Pipes, Mundra.
[5] Maheshwar Sahu retired as additional chief secretary, industries and mining, on 31 January,2014. I met him on 4 February, 2014 in Gandhinagar.

'Capital intensive' is a cuss phrase used by Leftists to disparage large private industries (never state-owned ones). Profit-orientation makes these corporations, in their imagination, industrial predators. But large plants are not densely-foliaged arboreal sprawls that choke the undergrowth. Rather, they are industrial nurseries. According to the 2010-11 annual survey of industries, Gujarat had 21,300 factories or ten percent of the country's total. These are large units where the average number of workers is more than fifty. Topping the list is Tamil Nadu with 17 percent of them. Gujarat ranks fourth, but a short gap separates it from the two states that are immediately ahead. Gujarat also employs a tenth of India's factory labour. This is proportionately more than second ranking Maharashtra, whose population is twice as large. Employment generated per crore rupees of investment and output has been falling in Gujarat, but unemployment rates are much lower there than in the country.

Being big business need not make a state difficult for small industries. In the engineering industry, large aggregators like car companies sit atop a chain of sub-assemblers and parts manufacturers. Gujarat has over two hundred industrial estates and they are thriving enclaves of small and medium enterprises. Even in process industries like petrochemicals, a lot of service jobs are created. And they attract converters of say plastic into pipes, sheets and other products. The state has nearly half a million micro and small enterprises. At the beginning of the last decade there were a little more than half as many.

∼

It is said that all birds lay eggs but it is only the hen that crows. Marketing is an essential tool for politicians. Modi is adept at the art. He knows that it is not enough to deliver on promises; he has to manage perceptions as well. Understatement is a virtue in a journalist. Modi does not belong to the Infosys school of under-promising and over-delivering. He knows he cannot under-sell and does not.

A former colleague at *India Today* who has known Modi for a long time, recalls him saying something like this when asked about this quirk: 'Is there anyone working harder than me, anyone who is more innovative or more meticulous? Then why should I not seek publicity?'

Advertising and public relations professional, Pankaj Mudholkar, the person behind the Vibrant Gujarat campaign says, 'Modi believes in visibly showcasing the tangibles.' He recalls Modi patting an official after a presentation for his department's good work but giving him 'zero marks' because few knew about it.

'He is good at branding,' acknowledges Sahu. 'That is how you activate everybody for a cause. If you do not do branding you cannot put energy the whole hog.'

Modi has not made Gujarat business-friendly. It has always been so. Upon becoming a state in 1960, it wanted to be richer than Maharashtra from which it had separated. In 1969, union commerce minister Manubhai Shah and V G Patel launched the 'Technician Scheme'. Shah was a graduate of Massachusetts Institute of Technology. As union commerce minister he helped set up Gujarat's Industrial Development Corporation and scores of industrial estates across the country. Patel was GIDC's economic adviser. The scheme was meant to train engineers in entrepreneurship as most of them lacked confidence, did not know to draft business plans, were ignorant about obtaining loans, or had little idea of managing enterprises.[6]

From this emerged in April 1970, the entrepreneurship development programme. Many years later Patel recalled[7] that

---

[6] Kamlesh Kanwar, *Icons of Gujarat Industry: Stories of Rare Grit and Enterprise*, Harmony Publishers, 2000.
[7] *The Rap of Enterprise*, *Outlook*, 11 October, 2012.

forty-five persons were invited for the inaugural session, but thirty-seven turned up. 'We had industrial estates, we set up an investment corporation to finance projects, but the entrepreneurs to take advantage of it all were missing,' Patel told *Outlook* magazine. In 1983, the Entrepreneurship Development Institute was set up as a national institution, with support from central government-owned investment banks. Within thirty years it had trained about 10,000 job creators.

Industrial Extension Bureau or iNDEXTb, an escort service for investors was another institution which Gujarat pioneered in 1977, and other states emulated. The first and last letters of the acronym are in lower case to convey that bloated egos (or I) and bureaucratic red tape would not be impediments as Gujarat sought to become India's preferred investment destination. The agency did not depend on the state budget for funding; that insulated it from political whim.

The head of the bureau had the rank of chief secretary and direct access to the chief minister. 'Its decisions were often ratified without demur,' says its first managing director, Jay Narayan Vyas, who is also the state BJP's face in television debates. An engineer and economist, Vyas held many portfolios including health and tourism in Modi's cabinet before defeat in the last Assembly elections. The agency's origin reveals how eager the bureaucracy was to facilitate business. During one of the weekly tea meetings at the industry commissioner's office, a custom said to have begun around 1972, Vyas, then an official, came up with the idea of a body that would provide 'industrial intelligence', to potential investors. The meetings used to be attended by the chief secretary, the finance secretary and managing directors of the state's various industrial promotion and financial corporations. The conversations were about investments. A cell was already in existence in the industries department for non-resident Indian investors. From their feedback, came the idea of a bureau that would liaise with various state agencies for clearances and concessions.

To help investors navigate the byzantine maze of the license permit raj, the state government posted a senior official in Delhi. It had offices in Mumbai, Kolkata and East Africa to meet and greet investors. iNDEXTb was quite systematic in monitoring letters of intent (LoIs) and their conversion into industrial licenses. It would procure a list of LoIs issued by the central government for Gujarat, and write to each investor inquiring whether they had applied for conversion of intent into licenses, and if so, where the application was stuck and for how long. The bureau would pursue the applications to their logical conclusion. Investors were also given a choice of industrial locations. One analysis showed that 60 percent of LoIs had been converted to industrial licenses between 1977 and 1985. Gujarat was rigorous in ensuring that project achievement targets were met. Subsidy was released only on the basis of progress made in production.

The bureau would disseminate information about profitable opportunities, conduct investment campaigns and reach out to prospective entrepreneurs — activities which Modi's flagship investment platform, Vibrant Gujarat does, except that the road shows which used to be held in metros and abroad (the first time in 1997), have now become a grand event centred in capital Gandhinagar. The bureau 'exists as a shell', laments Vyas implying that its role has diminished, though the chief minister leading the investment effort should be preferable to bureaucrats doing the canvassing.

Between 1974 and 1990, Gujarat was second in getting letters of intent. By the mid-eighties it had attained the third position in number of industries. Twenty-four of the country's 200 biggest companies were located in Gujarat.

Industrial promotion and the securing of investments has been consistent theme with all Gujarat governments since it became a state. The officials in charge virtually belonged to a special cadre. They had well-appointed offices and expense accounts, while the rest of their service had to abide by the ethic of Gandhian frugality. Road shows to attract investments were held not only in India but also abroad; the presence of a Gujarati expat community helped ease the pinch during the time of foreign exchange restrictions. Once economic reforms took root, the state regarded itself as a breakaway province of China in terms of growth rate. Singapore was regarded as a benchmark for investment facilitation. Officials were not squeamish about visiting industry leaders in their offices. 'We never had the boxwallah culture,' says Labanyendu Mansingh, a Gujarat cadre officer, who also served as India's Director-General of Foreign Trade. But chief ministers before Modi usually did not lead the investment effort from the front. Once a deal was stitched up, they would meet the investors for a courtesy chat.

Among Gujarat's chief ministers, Chimanbhai Patel set the trend of wooing investments aggressively. During his second stint of four years from March 1990, he facilitated a number of infrastructure and large industrial projects like the Reliance petrochemicals complex in Hazira. Patel bullied the coalition government at the centre for a generous supply of gas to the state, concessional prices, and higher royalties for oil. He persuaded Prime Minister Rajiv Gandhi's government to give the long-delayed environment clearance for the Narmada dam by cajoling environment secretary T N Seshan. Patel, wanted overnight decisions, says Nikita Sud, who looks at Gujarat's economic liberalization through the prism of Hindu Nationalism in a 2012 book.[8] A bureaucrat told Sud from personal acquaintance that Patel brooked no delays. He would regard necessary, but detailed, and therefore time-taking scrutiny

---

[8] Nikita Sud, *Liberalization, Hindu Nationalism and The State,* Oxford University Press, 2012.

of his proposals as an affront to Gujarati *asmita* or pride, a tactic, according to Sud, Patel had learnt from Andhra chief minister N T Rama Rao who was ever ready to brandish Telugu *atma gauravam*.

Patel was a risk-taker and would even bet on rookies. 'In a *bania* state think like a *bania*,' Nikhil Gandhi a pioneer port developer recalls Patel as telling his finance secretary in a display of Gujarati practicality. Gandhi, who owns a shipyard and joined hands with industrialist Mukesh Ambani to establish special economic zones (SEZ), had no experience in developing ports. Yet he offered to set up one in Pipavav, when the government invited private sector interest in ten ports. Those established by the centre, called 'major' ports, could not cope with demand. Gujarat realized ahead of the others that there was no ban on states setting up ports, and though officially these were called 'minor' there was no bar on how big they could get. The secretary suspected that Gandhi was an interloper, who would take concessions and arm-twist the government into offering more as construction progressed. If Gandhi scooted half way through, the government would have to clean up the mess. 'So what,' Patel reasoned, 'we will complete the project on our own. That way we will get a port at half the price!'

Being a state with India's longest coastline, port-led development is a cornerstone of Gujarat's development strategy. The state set up the country's first maritime board in 1982. Chimanbhai's private port initiative got institutionalized into port-led development under BJP chief ministers Keshubhai Patel and Suresh Mehta in 1995. They crafted policies and concession agreements to encourage private investment in the sector and set up the country's first infrastructure development board.

By the time Kesbhubhai stepped down and Modi took over in October 2001, Gujarat had got sizeable private investment in Pipavav, Mundra, Sikka and Dahej ports. Plans were afoot to restructure the electricity utility with money from the Asian

Development Bank. A ten-year infrastructure blueprint had been drawn up. There was a similar road map for the agriculture sector. The Supreme Court had allowed construction to resume on the long-delayed Narmada dam and had also given the green signal for it to be raised to full height provided environmental concerns were met and the rehabilitation of displaced persons was not neglected like before. A large number of check-dams had been constructed in parched Saurashtra and Kutch.

It is true that Modi has given shine to old metal. But he did not just slip into the cozy comfort of well-worn shoes after he took over; he has created his own legacy as well. Modi has propelled Gujarat's economy higher and in new directions. An uninterrupted tenure of more than a decade in a state known for revolving door chief ministers has given stability to policies. Clear thinking, decisive action, farsightedness, unbounded energy, innovative ideas and a strong focus on development have enabled Gujarat to enjoy more than a decade of near-double digit growth. There have been growth spurts during the tenures of earlier chief ministers — but not prolonged elevated spells.

∽

During Modi's career as chief minister, Gujarat has received the second largest number of investment intentions at 5,200, just after Maharashtra's 7,720 (thought these need not get converted into factories). In terms of proposed investment, Orissa and Chhattisgarh are higher up, but it is clunky investment in mining. Gujarat ranks third in investment pledges at Rs 10.07 lakh cr and the amount is spread over a larger number of projects.[9]

Development is Modi's best advertisement and defence. It is no coincidence that the first Vibrant Gujarat International Investment

---

[9] http://dipp.nic.in/English/Publications/SIA_Statistics/AnnualIssue/2012-13/chapter2.2.pdf.

Summit (tagline: Where Life is a Celebration) happened in 2003. That was nineteen months after the riots in which 1,044 people were killed, 790 of them Muslim, according to figures cited in Parliament. It has an uncanny parallel to the development of Shanghai as the 'dragonhead' of China's economy after the 1989 Tiananmen Square crackdown on students protesting for democracy in Beijing. China's liberalizer Deng Xiaoping had to shore up the legitimacy of the communist party after the massacre. The effect of Western sanctions had to be countered and the country's commitment to economic reforms affirmed to prevent an economic slowdown that would have stoked domestic discontent. Pudong, a 522 sq km expanse of paddy fields and swamps adjoining Shanghai was developed as a financial district with exceptional freedom and liberal tax concessions.

Though the ferocity of the Gujarat riots abated after a few days, the disturbances continued for many weeks, till police officer KPS Gill, known for his role in suppressing Sikh militancy in Punjab, was appointed security advisor. Gill said he did not sense any remorse. Gujarat Hindus seemed to largely approve of the killings as a justified reaction to the macabre burning on 27 February, 2002 of Hindutva *kar sevaks* (volunteers) returning from Ayodhya, by train after a *mahayagna* or grand ritual at the site of a sixteenth century mosque which had been razed by Hindu zealots in 1992 to correct a historical wrong.

Overwhelming support for Modi's government in the elections that followed the riots would have fizzled out if social unrest had disrupted business and caused economic pain. Government's failure at preventing the riots had pricked the conscience of even hard-nosed businessmen. National industry chamber FICCI, and its Gujarat chapter maintained a studied silence. But the Confederation of Indian Industry spoke out, mainly at the prodding of its members from Mumbai's Parsi community (which traces its roots to Gujarat) like Anu Aga, chairwoman of Thermax, an energy and environment engineering company and Cyrus Guzder, owner of a logistics business which was acquired by FedEx. Kolkata based industrialist and CII President Sanjeev Goenka, known to be close to the Congress, but belonging to a community that has traditionally supported Modi's party said, 'What is happening there and the way the situation is being handled is definitely not right. These kinds of things are bound to have a negative impact on investment climate in Gujarat and the country as a whole.'[10] Deepak Parekh, a highly-regarded Gujarati, and chairman of Housing Development Finance Corporation, spoke tough: 'Internationally we have lost our name as a secular country. I am ashamed to have seen this in our century. The chief minister must take responsibility and resign. If the powers in Delhi are supporting him, it is unacceptable. If politicians have prevented the police from doing their duties, it cannot be tolerated. Some heads have to roll.'[11]

At CII Gujarat's annual day in Ahmedabad, a month after the riots, Guzder broke 'with our customary practice of being politically correct' and addressed the question: 'Is secularism good for business?' He said that 'the business of business is business,' only if the 'business of government is government.' In his view, 'there are no minority or majority rights, only human rights.' Business 'can and must act,' Guzder asserted. 'It shall have to stop being a silent constituency and gather courage,' as HDFC's Deepak Parikh had done the previous day, he pointed out. It was a moving exposition of India's Constitutional values and why businesses should foster a liberal society as a virtue in itself, and also because it made economic sense.

Even a year later, the industry club had not come to terms with the riots. I remember being at Delhi's Le Meridien hotel as a reporter of CNBC-TV18 business news channel for a CII interaction with Modi on 6 February, 2003. A half-hour documentary called 'Gujarat:

---

[10] http://www.sabrang.com/gujarat/statement/trindi.htm. Accessed in February 2014.
[11] http://www.sabrang.com/gujarat/statement/trindi.htm. Accessed in February 2014.

the Sunshine State,' was screened. The tag line said: 'The state that runs like a company.' Industrialists Rahul Bajaj and Jamshyd Godrej broached the subject of law and order situation in Gujarat, and the values Modi stood for. 'One cannot help feel that the year 2002 from the point of view of economic development was somewhat of a lost year for Gujarat,' the outspoken Bajaj said. (His grandfather Jamnalal Bajaj believed in ethical business and gave away almost all his wealth for Gandhiji's ideals and objectives.)

Godrej declared that CII had evolved as an institution because it encouraged different views to be expressed. 'There can be no change in that policy. However, the disruption of meetings is something we cannot allow.'

Godrej was referring to an incident the previous month in Mumbai. CII had invited business leaders to listen to Modi's pitch on investment opportunities in Gujarat. The invitees were silent on the fallout of the riots. But the meeting was rudely interrupted by a group of anti-communal activists led by visiting Oxford University fellow Jairus Banaji, who had asked Modi whether justice could be shorn from governance?[12]

Modi reacted angrily at the use of *'teekhi'* (sharp) language at the Delhi meeting.[13] 'You and your pseudo-secular friends can come to Gujarat if you want an answer.' The state had attracted Rs 8,000 cr in investment over the previous eight months, 'so what are you asking me about law and order?'

'I am of the view that CII had over the past year done great injustice to Gujarat,' Modi asserted.[14] From Modi's aggression it was clear that CII could not get away with the affront. A month later, on

---

[12] Modi Gets Earful at CII function, *Times of India,* Mumbai, 19 January, 2003. Accessed on 18 March, 2014.

[13] Modi Clashes with Godrej, Bajaj, *Economic Times,* 7 February, 2003. Accessed on 18 March, 2014.

[14] My report on CNBC-TV18 filed on 7 Feburary, 2003. Tape No D 2140, VF EM 15:06:34.

7 March, its director-general Tarun Das flew to Gandhinagar and apologized for the hurt caused to the chief minister and the state.[15] Das was under pressure. Modi had boycotted its oil and gas industry exhibition. CII's local chapter was also reportedly planning to break away. The industrialists behind Nirma, Adani, Cadila, Ashima and Torrent under the banner of Resurgent Group of Gujarat had launched an offensive at 'a concerted attempt to tarnish the image of the state'.[16] They called the riots of the previous year as 'a social mishap' that should not be 'misused as a political yardstick.'

Manoj Mitta, in his book, *The Fiction of Fact-Finding: Modi and Godhra*, says Modi used the excuse of economic development to try and block the National Human Rights Commissions' attempt before the Supreme Court to shift reinvestigation of Baroda's Best Bakery case (in which fourteen persons were killed) to the Central Bureau of Investigation and hold the retrial outside Gujarat. In a letter to the President, he wrote: 'Vested interests are trying to obstruct the path of progress. They are identifying stray incidents and exaggerating them with the sole objective of slowing the pace of development.'

It was in this context that Maheshwar Sahu, then industries commissioner, along with D J Pandian, managing director of Gujarat State Petroleum Corporation and Arvind Sharma, the head of iNDEXTb had decided on an international investor meet. The objective was not so much as to secure investments as to erase the perception created by unrelenting coverage, especially in the national English media, that Gujarat was unsafe for business. Modi was cold to the idea at first but warmed up to it eventually. The three officials formed a core committee and were given a free hand. It was decided to host the first event in September 2003, nineteen

---

[15] CII says Sorry to Narendra Modi, *Times of India*, Ahmedabad edition, 7 March, 2003. Accessed on 18 March, 2014.
[16] State Businessmen Corner CII, *Times of India*, Ahmedabad edition, 20 February, 2003. Accessed on 18 March, 2014.

months after the riots. It coincided with Navratri, when Gujarat is at its liveliest and women out on streets late at night. FICCI, was rewarded for its silence on the riots with partnership of the event.

The title was borrowed from 2001 tourism campaign, Vibrant Gujarat: the Colours of India, created by a team from the advertising agency Grey Worldwide led by Pankaj Mudolkar, at the instance of C T Misra, the managing director of Gujarat Tourism. It projected the state as offering all of India — beaches, wilderness and wildlife, heritage spots and pilgrimages sites — in the span of a compact holiday.

Mudholkar says in the run up to the investment summit, a series of half-hour feature programmes were sponsored on the business news channel, CNBC-TV18. They showcased the state's strength and potential. Modi's quotes were mandatory. He spoke about his vision. The Hindi news channel Aaj Tak ran a paid clip called *'Desh Mein Navratri* brought to you by Vibrant Gujarat' in its prime time news bulletins. It showed the celebration of Navratri across the country. News magazines ran advertorials that looked like editorials, extolling Gujarat's business climate. The underlying message of these media campaigns was 'happy, happening Gujarat.'[17]

Shailesh Pathak, an investment banker who joined the Indian Administrative Service and quit as a secretary to the Chhatisgarh government to return to private investment banking and equipment finance has attended all Vibrant Gujarats except the first. He says they are 'like an Indian wedding where one effectively spends five minutes with the groom and his family and the rest of the time with friends.' The events have become a must-go because 'you meet everyone who matters in Indian business.'

Modi became a 'rockstar' according to Pathak, at the 2009 Vibrant Gujarat held at Science City in Ahmedabad in the second

---

[17] Based on a conversation with Pankaj Mudholkar.

week of January. There was a gloom over Indian business following the collapse of the leading US investment bank, Lehman Brothers, a few months before, in September 2008. The world's financial system had seized up; exports had shrunk because banks were not honouring letters of credit. The Sensex had fallen 52 percent within a year. The Indian government had given a stimulus to the economy worth Rs 186,000 cr or 3.5 percent of GDP in two installments within the space of a month in the forms of tax concessions and contracts (like orders for buses). And in October 2008, days after its Nano car plant was sent packing from Singur in West Bengal, Tata Sons Chairman Ratan Tata had walked into Modi's embrace and announced that it would be relocated at Sanand, near Ahmedabad. Modi was riding high. He had led his party to victory for the second time. He gave investors the cheer they sought. Their response was so good that the head of a large housing finance company commented that such an event would have been difficult to pull off in Mumbai.

Six biennial Vibrant Gujarat investment summits have been held so far. They are no longer government to business affairs. Investors use the platform for networking. A lot of business to business deals happen without the government entering the equation. The event has become Gujarat's window to the world. Countries like Japan and Canada have become event partners. Unlike in China where much of the investment is from overseas Chinese, the share of non-resident Gujarati investment has not exceeded single digits.[18]

Every event has been grander in scale than the previous one. They are meticulously planned with officials being assigned individual responsibility for various tasks. At the last summit, the government said about 18,000 investment intentions were received, against 8,400 in 2011. Over two thousand foreign delegates attended. The government did not play up the size of investment pledges because they do not mean much. In 2011, Modi had claimed that investment

---

[18] Maheshwar Sahu, April 2011.

commitments worth $450 billion had been received. This was almost equal to the Indian government's infrastructure investment target of half a trillion dollars for the entire five-year plan period ending 2012. A sizeable chunk of the pledges do not materialize. The investment hit rate for the first two events, according to an industry chamber and a newspaper, varied between a quarter and a third, against the official claim of 70 percent.

Even a third of the pledges getting converted into plant, machinery and jobs is not bad at all. Investor enthusiasm for Gujarat is not in doubt. In the twenty year period of 1991-2011, Gujarat received $7 billion in foreign direct investment. It ranks fourth on the list, sandwiched between Tamil Nadu and Andhra Pradesh. Mahatrashtra is way ahead with $44.5 billion and the Delhi region ranks second with $25 billion. His critics say this blows a giant hole in Modi's claim of Gujarat being a preferred investment destination. But Gujarat was lower down on the list at one time. What is important is not where it is, but where it has come from. Mumbai gets the most FDI because it is India's traditional commercial capital. As a political centre, Delhi is naturally attractive to investors. Chennai has colonial claims to being an industrial centre. Ahmedabad was the centre of India's textile industry. The polytechnic which the king of Baroda set up before Independence incubated a dyes and chemicals industry. But the state has to negotiate a higher degree of difficulty. It is not a natural draw for computer and financial services firms — industries that get a sizeable chunk of foreign investment. It also lacks the frills of life being staunchly vegetarian and officially a liquor-free zone.

∽

The chief minister as chief salesman is not uniquely a Modi formulation. The 1991 economic reforms gave states a greater role in attracting investments. This coincided with the weakening of Congress rule at the centre and the era of coalitions. Andhra's Chandrababu Naidu epitomized the chief minister as CEO of the state: meeting US President Bill Clinton and Microsoft founder Bill Gates, making presentations at Davos, and swaying marquee information technology investments to transform the state capital into Cyberabad.

In his book *Plain Speaking*,[19] Naidu recounts how he wanted an exclusive meeting with Gates but was invited as part of a herd. Prevailing on US Ambassador Frank Wisner, Naidu, on whose Telugu Desam Party, Prime Minister Atal Behari Vajpayee's government was dependent, managed a one-on-one. Naidu made an impressive sales pitch and wowed Gates with offers of partnership in the Indian Institute of Information Technology, a strategic tie-up with AP Technology Services and a software development centre, for which China and Israel were competing. Naidu got construction company Larsen & Toubro to build Hi-Tech City in just fifteen months. That was a coup, Naidu says. It raised Andhra's investment quotient and pulled up its ranking in investor perception from twenty-second in 1995 to second in 2000.

Naidu says in his book that a chief minister and his officials cannot be like rulers; they must be enablers and facilitators. 'A politician who wants to deliver cannot have an ego. He has to lobby the central government for funds, using every persuasion he can think of. He has to woo industry and sell his state as an attractive investment destination. He has to woo foreign investment. He has to impress upon funding agencies that he can deliver.'

The late Murasoli Maran was another political leader in the tradition of Naidu, and anticipated Modi. He was unlike his uncle M Karunanidhi, former chief minister of Tamil Nadu and leader of the Dravida Munnetra Kazhagham party, who like his successor

---

[19] N Chandrababu Naidu and Sevanti Ninan, *Plain Speaking*, Penguin, 2000.

J Jaylalithaa behaves like the feudal ruler Naidu warned against. Maran as union commerce minister in 1996 used the life support which the DMK gave the National Front government along with cheap land, tax sops and assured power to pull the Ford car factory to Tamil Nadu over Maharashtra's claim. His son Dayanidhi Maran as telecom minister in the Congress-led United Progressive Alliance's first term in office, secured investments from Sony, Samsung, Dell and Nokia. 'We have made Chennai a perfect ecosystem for electronic manufacturers,' Maran boasted in 2007.

Naidu and Modi's styles have much in common, though there are significant departures as well. Both believe in method and planning. Naidu had set up a school to train party cadre, modelled on the one pioneered by an Oxford educated farmer leader who was the subject of his doctoral thesis: N G Ranga, founder of the Swatantra Party which rejected socialism and cooperative farming. Like Modi's vision documents, Naidu produced a twenty-year economic blueprint by engaging management consultancy McKinsey. Both have reformed state enterprises; Modi by insulating them from political interference, Naidu by selling the loss-making ones. Both believe in e-governance. A visit to the temple town of Tirupati and a brush with its computerized system of giving appointments for *darshan* of the presiding deity Lord Venkateswara, became Naidu's inspiration for e-Seva centres, where utility bills could be paid and government certificates obtained. Gujarat's Jan Seva Kendras are similar but their inspiration was a cricket match and a collector's desire to make the district administration more responsive. The extensive use of videoconferencing is another common quirk. Modi is a champion of public private partnerships; Naidu's AP Idea (infrastructure development enabling act) 2001 was meant to promote PPPs.

While Naidu reveled in his image as a CEO, Modi has not fallen for it. He may behave like one, and the video he showed businessmen in 2003 pitched Gujarat as a 'state that runs like a company,' but he does not like to be called that. When I asked him in a 2008 interview whether his style of setting performance targets and chasing them was not like that of a CEO, he said it was 'because this is the 21st century,' but 'I do not think I am a leader... I am a soldier of the state.'

While Naidu's party was plagued with corruption and he may have come across as cold, distant and corporatist to voters — reasons perhaps for his shock defeat, Modi's government is seen as relatively clean (but not corruption-free). He keeps his family at a distance. Being single Modi says he has no compulsion to amass wealth to bestow on his children.

And he has not neglected agriculture. In fact, he has invested in it. Naidu believed that incomes could not rise rapidly without growth in industry and services. Naidu's electricity reforms and tariff raises happened during a period of prolonged drought, and angered farmers; Modi provides assured but rationed supply daily for a few hours to farm pumps. He did not hesitate to imprison power thieves. But farmers are grateful because their incomes have improved.

The way Naidu got the Indian School of Business (ISB) located in Hyderabad reminds one of Modi's pursuit of the Nano car factory. When a financial daily reported that ISB was having difficulties with the Maharashtra government, Naidu rang up Anil Ambani, who was heading a five-man committee, and made generous offers which they could not refuse.[20]

Similarly, when the Nano car factory was caught in a political crossfire at Singur in West Bengal between Mamata Banerjee's Trinamool Congress and the Left front government over land acquisition, Rata Tata, fearing for the safety of his employees and managers decided to close down the partially-built factory. When

---

[20] Naidu's Andhra Pips State to Post; Bags Elite Business-school Project, 7 September, 1995, www.expressindia.com. Accessed on 14 Feb, 2014.

Modi came to know about this, he sent a text message to Tata's saying *'suswagatam'* or welcome. When Tata took up the offer, Modi went all out. He gave Tata Motors 1,100 acres of land at Sanand near Ahmedabad at less than the market price, payable in installments. News reports said the price was Rs 400 cr, or a little less than Rs 900 a square metre. Exemption from stamp duty, a postponement of value-added tax, infrastructures like roads, drainage and power, a large loan on a very low rate of interest, added up to a sizeable package. The entire deal was stitched up in less than a month.[21] Gujarat government officials said they were in touch with Tata Motors executives even before, with Niira Radia, head of the PR firm Vaishnavi Communications, playing the broker. Sahu, who was industries secretary, says the concessions must be seen as investment; they will payback many times over. Tata said it was 'a homecoming'. The allusion was perhaps to the factory site, which was the location of a cattle farm established with a donation from the group's founder during the famine of 1900. 'I have to say there is no state like Gujarat,' Tata said. It was quite the endorsement which Modi was looking for. The Tatas have a reputation for ethical behaviour and employee welfare. The shy and understated Ratan Tata commands public respect which very few Indian corporate leaders enjoy. 'I hope that there is a bad "M" and a good "M". We need that transition,' Tata said while taking questions from the press, with Modi seated next to him.[22]

From investment facilitation to investment solicitation, there has been a paradigm shift over the years. Big investors want to meet the Chief Minister because they seek to gain perspective and obtain assurances for the future, says Sahu. Business promotion has become an important aspect of diplomacy as well.

---

[21] Tata announced withdrawal from Singur on 3 September, 2008 and formally declared Sanand was the new location on 3 October.
[22] I hope there's a good 'M' and a bad 'M', says Tata, www.rediff.com/money. 8 October, 2008. Accessed on 14 February, 2014.

In October 2012, UK High Commissoner James Bevan met Modi ending a ten-year boycott. On 13 February, 2014 US Ambassador Nancy Powell met Modi in Gandhinagar 'as part of the US Mission's outreach to senior leaders of India's major political parties in advance of the upcoming national elections,' the embassy's press release said. It signalled a thaw between the two after the US had revoked a visa to Modi in 2005 under a law barring entry to foreign officials seen as responsible for 'severe violations of religious freedom.'

From political untouchable to a sought after leader, Modi's journey has been remarkable. The cult of development had made him acceptable.

3. New Charms for Agriculture

Offbeat ideas — a few of them quite radical, receptivity to novel technologies like Bt cotton and an unconventional approach to taking them to the countryside has ignited enterprise in farmers. This makes Gujarat's growth pro-poor.

Parthi Chaudhary was a police official with the Anti-Corruption Bureau posted at Mehsana in Gujarat when I met him in Ahmedabad's Rajpath Club in May 2013. He was in the news for busting records not scams. Three years before, in March 2010, his crop of potatoes, called Lady Rosetta after their light pink peel, yielded 87.188 tons a hectare. The sampling and assessment, Chaudhary says, was done by a team assigned by district collector R J Patel. It comprised agricultural experts from nearby Dantiwada University. A senior executive of McCain Food, which has a factory in Mehsana and supplies potato products to McDonald's, the American fast food chain, supports the claim. This is supposed to be a world record not in terms of absolute harvest, but factoring India's shorter potato season and fewer sunshine hours.[1] India's best average yield, from Gujarat and Punjab, is 26 tons a hectare.

---

[1] According to Gopal Dass Sharma, senior procurement officer of McCain Foods (India), Europe's potato season is of 120-140 days against India's 90 days. Europe gets 12-14 hours of sunshine a day compared to India's nine. So while European farms have yielded harvests of 120 tons a hectare, Parthi Chaudhary's is regarded as a record; he got the yield with fewer sunshine hours. A Google search throws up another claimant from Bihar, who is said to have harvested 108.8 tons per hactare in 2013 without inorganic fertilizer which is difficult to believe. This story appeared in *Forbes India* on 2 August 2013.

Chaudhary treats his ninety-acre farm like nature's manufactory. For him agriculture is an industrial activity which can be broken up into discrete processes that play up the aspects that aid growth and tamp down those that do not, to coax out the best that a crop can give. His employees are partners in the venture: they get a share of the produce under the prevalent practice of *bhagidhari* (sharing). To win them over to his management style, Chaudhary has devised a matrix of 100 points. A score of 70 plus gets a bonus; below 50 percent earns a penalty. So far there have been only winners.

Lady Rosetta is a variety high in solids and low in sugar, which Chaudhary cultivates for Rajkot's Balaji Wafers. He is also a supplier to PepsiCo. For French fries at McDonald's, the preferred varieties are long, not round, like Innovator and Kennebec. At the time of our conversation, Chaudhary had 1,400 tons in cold storage. He got a yield of sixty-seven tons a hectare that year. At the prevailing price of Rs 14 a kg the stock was worth Rs 1.96 cr. That is a cool 300 percent return in just 120 days on an investment of Rs 52 lakh.

Banaskantha has known potato farming from colonial days, but it is Canada's McCain Foods, the family-owned global supplier to McD's, and a seller of own-brand wedges, fries and *tikkies*, that has taught the district's farmers how to grow them scientifically. McCain followed McD's to India in 1998. It worked on potatoes in Punjab, Haryana and Uttar Pradesh but found the cold weather there inhibiting weight gain in tubers and raising their levels of sugar (which caramelizes and turns fries dirty brown). West Bengal, like Gujarat, has the ideal climate, but plot sizes are too small for contract farming, so it gave up trials there.

McCain found enormous waste in Gujarat. Flood irrigation was the practice; the water flushed into the fields would add up to a 750 mm column by end of the crop season. Potatoes need moisture not drenching. Just as much water should be replenished as evaporates from soil and transpires through leaves. Farmers lavished nitrogen fertilizer to make up for the nutrient leaching through the sandy soil. High humidity brought pest and fungal attacks.

McCain persuaded farmers to use sprinklers, cutting water and nitrogen use by a third. They are commonplace now aided by government subsidies, and eight-hour rationed power supply to the farm grid. Late afternoon, Banaskantha's fields, enveloped in whispery mists and rainbow hues, are a sight to see. How long the sprinklers should be operational is determined by data provided by the company's two weather stations, one at a spot on way to Mt Abu, and the other at Himmatnagar in neighbouring Sabarkantha district. Through phone calls and text messages field staff conveys the information to farmers. Other innovations have reduced planting time, and energy use in cold storages.

McCain began contract farming in 2006 with four farmers and 16 acres in Badgam village. During my visit seven years later, 900 of them assured the company the produce of 4,500 acres. The landholdings in Banaskantha are quite big. Half the farmers own more than ten acres. But everyone, small or big, is invited to be a supplier, says procurement officer Gopal Dass Sharma, who is known to be free with agronomic advice even to farmers not on contract. The company's plant has an appetite of 50,000 tons a year, most of which is mopped up from within the vicinity. In November, at the beginning of the potato season farmers sign a contract pledging to supply potatoes equal to at least ten times the quantity of seed they receive from the company, by the third week of March, after which purchases stop. The quality parameters are specified; a detailed schedule of farming practices in Gujarati for each variety of potatoes is provided. Farmers are advised to think safety while spraying chemicals. They are told not to contaminate the potatoes with sewage water. Agronomic advice is also available on call. Farmers get seed spuds for half the price; the rest is deducted from the sale price. If farmers default, post-dated cheques are encashed.

Farmers start with McCain and, like Parthi Chaudhary, move on within a few years, after they get a hang of the art. Often they grow for multiple buyers. Unlike McCain, PepsiCo and Balaji Wafers buy through agents, who are paid a fee for seed supplied and potato procured at a price announced at the beginning of the season. These vendors dip into the open market if procurement falls short of contracted quantity.

An amalgam of factors — a law that allows farmers to sell directly to companies rather than through *mandis*; a choice of buyers, a rash of cold storages incentivized by subsidies and regular power supply; a network of good rural roads, and access to information on the Internet and the mobile phone — has given farmers better prices — and control over their lives.

The narrative of agriculture as a basket case; of farmers ruthlessly exploited by rapacious Indian and foreign capitalists; agrarian crisis brought about by globalization; and a countryside stalked by suicidal deaths, breaks down in Gujarat's potato belt. Small farmers like Manjibhai Chaudhary have gone entirely commercial. He buys wheat from the market, rather than himself growing it. From one-and-a-half acres to thirteen, he has been won over completely by potatoes.

His neighbour Meghrajbhai Chaudhary finds potato cultivation *'majedaar'*, (fun) proof of which is the thirty of thirty-five acres devoted to the crop. Prosperity allows him to indulge idiosyncracies like a 'farmhouse' built atop a thirty-foot high godown for a vantage view of fields.

Farmers like Kantibhai Becharbhai Patel try to maximize earnings by growing for two companies: one for assured income and the other to skim the cream if prices jump. A post-graduate in rubber and plastic technology, he finds corporates better at spreading agricultural technology than government agencies, because of aligned interests. They, like him, are keen to boost yield. His has gone up by a third to forty-five tons a hectare with their advice. This has made him a votary of privatization and foreign direct investment in retailing.

With agriculture profitable, youth have taken a shine to it. Bhavesh Saini, a student of chemical engineering from Nirma Institute of Technology, prefers farming to a salaried job. Originally from Haryana, he finds cultivating the family holding of sixty acres 'creative'. He is commercially monogamous; married to McCain so he can 'concentrate on production', though he finds the company's seed rather expensive. Saini does not care for subsidies so long as the government 'maintains the water table'.

Sumit Joshi of Daniya village, is another youth from a family of cultivators who had taken to 'systematic farming' in the past two years, after shutting down his business of trading in farm inputs. He owns less than five acres, but boosts bargaining clout through collective action by joining hands with a dozen friends when approaching buyers in the open market. So they have not felt the need for cooperatives or farmer producer companies.

∼

Studies by economist Ashok Gulati, formerly chairman of the central government commission that fixes agricultural support prices, have shown that growth in agriculture is more effective in reducing poverty than growth in industry or services. In China, poverty declined from 33 percent of the population in 1978 to 15 percent in 1984 — during the early part of the reforms — when agriculture grew by 7.1 percent a year. India's Green Revolution between 1960 and 1980 also caused a rapid decline in poverty.[2] The 140 million people pulled out of poverty during the ten years of UPA rule at the centre was in large measure caused by real agricultural GDP per worker rising 51 percent during these years

---

[2] Ashok Gulati and Shenggen Fan, editors, *The Dragon & The Elephant, Agricultural and Rural Reforms in China and India*, Oxford University Press, 2007.

on account of private investment and an absolute decline in the numbers engaged in farming.[3]

The farmer-corporate compact that one sees in Gujarat's potato belt, with the government playing facilitator, is one of the many ways of ushering in rural prosperity, just as the Amul milk cooperative model has done. For Gulati, a model's success depends on whether it is CISS-able. Banskantha's potato farming meets the criteria. It is competitive: higher yields allow farmers to earn more per acre despite low unit prices which companies seek. It is inclusive, as small farmers are not barred. If farm sizes inhibit deployment of machines, the government can help by easing the law on leasing. The model is scalable as increasing consumption of fries and wafers raises demand for potatoes. And it is sustainable, because water conserving technology, cold storages that save energy by operating at eight degrees centigrade instead of zero degrees, and the practice of providing just those nutrients to plants as are necessary on agronomic advice from corporates, enables more to be extracted out of less.

India's first Green Revolution was from 'seed to grain.' The second has to be from 'soil to market.' Agriculture can no longer be a subsistence activity. It has to be conducted like a business, with farmers growing what consumers want through direct linkages with retailers. The emphasis has to be on productivity, which can ensure higher income per acre for farmers while lowering the cost per kilogram to consumers. This means sowing high technology seeds; using fertilizer, water and pesticides judiciously; deploying machines to reduce drudgery and labour cost; and employing risk mitigation devices like crop insurance.

Gujarat is among the few states to allow (in 2005) traders, processors, and organised retailers to buy agricultural produce

---

[3] India's Second Green Revolution, *Financial Express*, 11 February, 2014.

directly from farmers without going through *arhatias* or commission agents. It has permitted spot exchanges to be set up. Companies can buy crop a year in advance. There is provision for paying extra if prices rise at the time of harvest. This has expanded the areas under contract cultivation. But the state has not permitted foreign organized retailers to open up stores in Gujarat, after the Central Government permitted FDI in retailing in 2012, in deference to the BJP's national policy (itself an U-turn from its earlier stand).

∽

Gujarat's agriculture is the real surprise in its development story. In the twelve years to 2011-12, it has grown at 8 percent a year, compared to 3.1 percent nationally. This is on par with neighbouring Rajasthan, but much faster than Maharashtra and Madhya Pradesh, with whom it shares borders. Bihar and Chhattisgarh's agricultural growth is in double digits, but Gujarat is water scare with regional disparities in distribution of rain.[4] The clouds are a quarter as generous on Kutch in the north as on the southern districts. Droughts were frequent in the past; this made the state's growth quite volatile. Growth was negative in seventeen of forty years after it became a separate state.

How has this happened? A combination of fortuitous circumstances like good monsoons; court approval for work on a lifeline dam to resume; the commercial approval of genetically-modified cotton seed; public investment in roads, power and canal irrigation; community participation in water conservation through check dams and micro-irrigation; and market-oriented policies combined with the innate enterprise of the Gujarati farmer have led

---

[4] Gujarat's average annual agricultural growth between 2001 and 2012 was 7.99 percent, that of Rajasthan 8.27 percent, Madhya Pradesh's 4.56 percent and Maharastra's 4.39 percent. Bihar leads with 12.37 percent growth, and Chhattisgarh is close behind at 11.43 percent. Planning Commission data.

to this happy situation. Some of these were works in progress when Modi stepped into office; others have been his initiatives.

Irrigation is clearly a major factor. The game changer has been the Narmada dam. This project was stalled for many years because of activists who wanted displaced tribals to be first rehabilitated and the height restricted so that fewer habitations would be submerged. But a severe drought in the late 1980s triggered a pro-dam agitation. Chief Minister Chimanbhai Patel cashed in on it and cajoled the centre into giving environmental clearance. In 1999, two years before Modi became chief minister, the Supreme Court allowed work to resume on condition that project-affected persons were taken care of. The dam is now sixteen metres short of target. It can be built to its full height provided the dam control authority is assured that those displaced in neighbouring Madhya Pradesh and Maharashtra will be properly relocated.[5] Once that is done, farmers in parched Saurashtra will get enough water for two crops instead of one. The dam can irrigate 3,100 villages, three quarters of them drought-prone, in fifteen districts. Much of the water still runs into the sea. The main canal is done; work on branches has been substantially completed. But only a third of the channels taking water to the fields have been laid. Work has been tardy in the past decade because of difficulties in acquiring land.[6] Of the 1.8 million hectares that the Narmada can irrigate in Gujarat, the full benefit is available only to one fifth of the area.[7]

Tushaar Shah, an economist who specializes in water issues, says farmers should be allowed to lay underground pipes to take water to fields. According to his survey, there has been a huge increase in

---

[5] Lok Sabha reply on 6 February, 2014: approval from the environmental sub-committee has been received but not from the R&R sub-group.
[6] Doomed Dam of Gujarat, *Hindustan Times*, May, 2013. Of 75,000 km canal network, only 26,000 km has been paid, 10,000 km of it in the past decade.
[7] www.sardarsarovardam.org

pump sales along the canal areas, despite a law making water theft an offence. His advice: 'go with the flow rather than resist it.'

Complementing this is a vigorous two decades old campaign to store rain water. The movement began after a severe three-year dry spell between 1985 and 1988 when drinking water had to be brought to Rajkot by train. Social workers gave impetus to it. A diamond merchant set up a trust in Saurashtra and conducted a 325 km foot-march in 1999 to popularize rain water conservation. The governments under Modi and his predecessor stepped in thereafter encouraging NGOs and the community. They gave financial grants and technical help like satellite maps to locate check dams and a set of designs to choose from. About 1.5 lakh check dams have been built across the state.[8]

Not only has water availability increased; drip and sprinkler irrigation is enabling Gujarat's farmers to extract more crop from every drop. The evocatively named Gujarat Green Revolution Company (GGRC) has given impetus to these water-saving technologies. It is not a pioneer though. Way back in 1991, the central government initiated a scheme. It got a boost subsequently from Atal Behari Vajpayee's government because of Andhra's progressive chief minister Chandrababu Naidu, an ally, who was converted to it after a visit to Israel. Subsidies were provided to persuade farmers but did not make much headway, except in states like Maharashtra. The mistake was in selling equipment and not the benefits. Farmers would take the subsidy and then junk the equipment, which had good resale price being of aluminum.[9]

Modi also got inspired after a visit to Israel but decided to implement micro-irrigation through a state-owned company, rather than a government department. Farmers have to pay their

---

[8] Socio economic review 2012-13.
[9] Shyamal Tikadar, former MD of Gujarat Green Revolution Company in a conversation in April 2011.

share upfront to be eligible for subsidy. The design and quality of equipment is approved by the governement; it varies according to crop. The presence of a large number of suppliers exerts competitive pressure on prices. The government pays its contribution electronically to check corruption; there are no cash transfers. Third party auditors visit fields to verify whether the equipment has actually been installed and that farmers are satisfied. Equipment suppliers are required to appoint agronomists to advice farmers on how to get the best benefit; the focus is on outcomes. The targets are monitored by the chief minister. 'When I see farmers prospering, I get the inertia (meaning, inspiration) to do more,' said Shyamal Tikadar, who headed GGRC at one time.

The availability of groundwater has been matched by the rationing of quality power to farm pumps. Gujarat farmers used to get power for about twenty hours daily in the 1980s. The introduction of a flat tariff towards end of that decade damaged the finances of the state utility. In 1999-2000, it ran losses of Rs 2,200 cr. The duration of rural supply fell to twelve hours a day. It was also erratic; there were frequent outages and brownouts which damaged the pumps. To cope, farmers would use capacitors, known locally as *totas*, which affected supply further down the line. The government preceding Modi's wanted to restructure the state power utility. A foreign loan had been contracted, but resistance from farmers to metering had held up the exercise.

Modi's masterstroke was to divide the rural grid into two, one of them subsidized and exclusively for pumps, and the other to homes and establishments, at a cost of nearly Rs 1,200 cr. The pump grid was assured of eight hours of quality power daily between specified non-peak hours, including nights every alternate week. A flat rate based on pump capacity was charged. Metering and charging according to actual use was not only logistically difficult, it would also have met with fierce resistance, as farmers find meter readers to be corrupt. The changed system was marketed as an exercise to help farmers and not to squeeze them. Women and school children voted for the bifurcation of feeders as homes would get power round the clock.

The experiment was tried out in eight districts in 2003, including poor Dangs and prosperous Anand where the water table was high. By November the next year, all villages were covered. The Anand-based International Water Management Institute (IWMI) claims ownership of this concept. It says it had made presentations to the top officials of the state power utility, the power minister and to the electricity regulator during 2001-02.[10]

But Modi tells Nilanjan Mukhopadhyay that 'the idea of separating the rural grid came to him as a revelation.' I think it is probably a god-gifted ability .... Like for instance, the solar panel on top of a canal (launched in the summer of 2012).... Even the Jyotigram Yojana — giving directions to separate the agricultural feeder and domestic feeder. Now I am not a technical person — and no one gave me this suggestion, it just came to my mind — why can't we do this. ... If you look at the file, for one year the entire file had nothing but rejection notes from various departments. All weighing ten kgs (laughs). No one was willing to agree with me.... Now we are getting kudos from the entire country because of this.'[11]

I P Gautam, who was collector of Rajkot, an assembly constituency where Modi won from in February 2002, and a power ministry official at launch of Jyotigram denies knowledge of the IWMI proposal. He says the idea was Modi's original. Tushaar Shah of IWMI admits he did not make any presentation to Modi. It is possible that Modi heard it tangentially from an official whom

---

[10] *Real-time Co-management of Electricity and Groundwater: An assessment of Gujarat's pioneering 'Jyotigram' scheme* by Tushaar Shah and Shilpa Verma, International Water Management Institute, Anand.
http://publications.iwmi.org/pdf/H041811.pdf
[11] *Narendra Modi: the Man, the Times*, Tranquebar, 2013.

IWMI had briefed, but forgot that he had. Shah also says that some non-resident Indians who had established a housing colony in Anand had told farmers to set up a separate feeder line for pumps at their own expense, so that homes would be spared the brownouts of a common line. Modi may have picked up that buzz. It is also quite likely that Modi and IWMI independently arrived at the same solution. Such coincidences are not uncommon in the history of innovation and scientific discovery.

The switch was not a smooth affair. The move to raise tariffs to a uniform Rs 800 per horsepower, though well short of the cost, was resisted by farmers, including those of the RSS-affiliated union. But Modi did not give in. Anti-theft legislation was enacted and many power thieves were jailed.

The scheme has resulted in multiple winners. Modi says children can study better because lights do not go off; school results have improved. Studies show that rural life has become more comfortable; this has reduced the pressure to migrate to cities. Shops, schools and hospitals can function with fewer interruptions. Non-farm activity has increased as establishments like garages, welding outfits, flour mills and oil presses are assured of power. Lesser time on domestic chores like grinding or drawing water, has enabled women to take up income-yielding work as activities like diamond polishing have shifted to villages.[12] Rationing of pump supply gives the government control over groundwater extraction. Between 2001 and 2006, electricity used by pumps fell by 37 percent. The government's farm subsidy bill has been pared and the state utility is making profits.

Farmers are satisfied but not exactly overjoyed. Their pumps are more reliable; breakdowns have decreased considerably. But there

---

[12] Real-time Co-management of Electricity and Groundwater: An assessment of Gujarat's pioneering 'Jyotigram' scheme, Tushaar Shah and Shilpa Verma, International Water Management Institute, Anand.
http://publications.iwmi.org/pdf/H041811.pdf

is resentment that power supply is for lesser duration than the promised eight hours. Night time provision is not only irksome but can also be unsafe. Landless farmers who cultivated leased fields with purchased water are the worst sufferers as informal water markets have either dried up, or the price of water has risen especially in areas were the water table is low and well recharge takes time.

They have another grouse; instead of varying the duration of supply according to irrigation requirement, power is given uniformly across the year. Farmers need power for a longer time for four to six weeks in a year, when crops are the thirstiest. There is also opposition to metering of new tube wells, which is mandatory.

∽

A vigorous debate had broken out a couple of years ago in the *Economic and Political Weekly*, with one set of academicians lauding Gujarat's 'agrarian miracle,' and another set providing ammunition to 'explode' the 'myth.' Comparing crop data for six years till 2005-06 with the previous seven years, Tushaar Shah and his team held the groundwater recharge movement in dry Saurashtra, Kutch and north Gujarat responsible for the state's high agricultural performance. While that period saw a succession of good monsoons, there was no big increase in rain-fed Kharif output, they said. The crop area, yield and profit margins in south and central Gujarat, which get the most rainfall, did not see any significant change. The doubling of the state's wheat output and a three-and-a-half fold increase in cotton production was due to expansion of irrigated area, and yield increases due to supplementary watering from tube wells.[13]

But the team interrogating these findings led by Dinesh Kumar of a Hyderabad-based institute said six years was too short a time

---

[13] Tushaar Shah et al, *Secret of Gujarat's Agrarian Miracle After 2000, Economic and Political Weekly*, 26 December 2009.

to make any inferences about Gujarat's agriculture. The 'miracle' was the result of a drought year being chosen as the base, which had inflated subsequent growth. But it agreed that Gujarat's agriculture had made 'significant strides' in the 2000s.

The increase in crop production, the Hyderabad researchers said, was due to the main Narmada canal, which had emptied water into dry rivers along its path raising water tables in the process. Crop production had also increased along the canal for the same reason. Though last-mile channels were yet to be built, farmers were pumping water into tankers and transporting them to fields. Though they were beyond the reach of canals, good monsoons had recharged aquifers in Saurashtra, Kutch and north Gujarat. Higher soil moisture had reduced dependence on pumped water.[14]

But both teams agreed that the reliance on groundwater was imprudent. Groundwater was fast depleting and pumping costs were a burden on the state. Dams were storing five billion cubic metres (bcm) of water but were irrigating only 6.5 lakh hectares, while farmers were using 11.5 bcm of groundwater to irrigate 27.5 lakh hectares. Gujarat must rethink its water strategy, Shah's team said. It must 'bank' a portion of its dam water in hard rock underground storages as Australia had successfully done.

The Hyderabad team questioned whether recharging of aquifers with harvested rainwater was actually helping increase water availability, in the absence of hydrological studies. While water saving was essential, it said the state should take quick steps to utilize dam water, which could turn the dry regions as prosperous as canal-irrigated south and central Gujarat.

That controversy had ideological overtones with the pro- and anti-Modi camps choosing the study best fitting their viewpoints.

---

[14] *Gujarat's Agricultural Growth Story: Exploding Some Myths* by M Dinesh Kumar, A Narayanamoorthy, OP Singh, MVK Sivamohan, Manoj Sharma and Nitin Bassi of Institute for Resource Analysis & Policy, March 2010.

Moving away from that digression to the main narrative of this chapter, the gains from the provision of water and electricity would not have been fully realized if Gujarat had not invested in roads. Leaders have been unmade by their inattention to *Bijli, Sadak, Paani*. In 2003, despite his investment in social infrastructure, Congress chief minister Digvijaya Singh famously lost Madhya Pradesh because of the pathetic state of roads. And one of the first things that Nitish Kumar did after becoming chief minister of Bihar in 2005, apart from restoring law and order, was to embark on a programme of road construction.

Gujarat always had a good network of roads, but in the past decade it has seen a big increase in paved ones. These were most likely village roads, as those in urban areas would have been the first to be paved. The village road network is a third of the total. Practically the entire network is paved.[15] Gujarat scores over most states in length and density. That is the reason it has been a pioneer in cooperative milk production. Studies have shown that a rupee investment in roads raises agricultural GDP by Rs 7.66 (second only to investment in agricultural R&D) and is best as reducing rural poverty.[16]

Roads have been at the top of mind of successive chief ministers. In 1981, Gujarat announced a twenty-year plan mainly for development of village roads with World Bank funds. In 2001, it launched a flagship road building programme for state-wide corridors, divided carriage ways in towns, village linkages to agriculture produce markets, and quick access to tourist destinations. Prime Minister Atal Behari Vajpayee saw himself as a road builder. In 1999, he laid the foundation for the Golden Quadrilateral to connect metros with

---

[15] According to the state's 2012-13 socio-economic review, the village road network, at 25,000 km, was a third of the total. The length of national highways went up by 1,200 km while that of state highways declined by about as much.

[16] By Shenggen Fan, Ashok Gulati and Sukhadeo Thorat quoted in 'Reforming Agriculture,' article in Seminar.

wide highways and the following years he launched a countrywide scheme to link villages with roads that could be used at all times. This has had a rub-off on the state. Its national highway length has gone up by a third.

Road development in Gujarat has benefited from institutional reforms. Much of the work is contracted out; procurement is done online. Rebidding is not unknown if cartelization is suspected. Annual plans are prepared on the basis of information thrown up by a computerized road management system. There is an 80/20 approach to maintenance, that is, 20 percent of the network which carries 80 percent of traffic gets priority in maintenance. International construction norms are followed. The computerization of land records has helped land acquisition (by ensuring that relief and rehabilitation reach the right people). The World Bank even commented appreciatively and has documented its experience as a lesson for other states.[17]

Apart from the improvement in physical infrastructures, Gujarat's agriculture has gained from its effort at putting scientific knowledge to sweat. In 2004, the four campuses of Gujarat Agriculture University were converted into as many independent universities. With greater autonomy came more funding for research and farm outreach. The following year, the annual Krishi Mahotsav was launched to revitalize the agricultural extension system, which had gone to seed after the World Bank pioneered 'training and visit' model of the Green Revolution era had become defunct. Since then every year, before the onset of monsoons, the entire administration is galvanized — ministers, officials of eighteen departments, scientists and village workers — for a month long exercise in agricultural outreach. Braving the summer heat they visit each of the state's 18,000 villages. About 200 Krishi Raths

---

[17] Institutional Development and Good Governance in the Highway Sector – Learning from Gujarat, The World Bank, 2011.

(agriculture chariots) replete with audio-visual equipment, posters and soil testing equipment are deployed. Soil health cards are given, and farmers are advised about ways to restore fertility, the best-suited crops to grow and the livestock activity to be undertaken. Agriculture loans are disbursed, and cattle vaccinated. In addition, agricultural colleges and agriculture science centres (or Krishi Vigyan Kendras) organize *melas* to bridge the knowledge gap, which are attended by hundreds of farmers.

Finally, it is the innate enterprise of Gujarati farmers and their desire to prosper that compels the initiatives listed above and flatters their outcomes. The potato case study elaborated at the beginning of this chapter is not an exception. The desire to try out new things is ingrained in the Gujarati psyche. This is best illustrated by the example of Bt cotton, a variety resistant to attacks from the boll weevil, because of a toxic gene extracted from a soil bacterium, and grafted through genetic manipulation.

Bt cotton was, and remains, the only genetically-modified seed approved for sale in India. In April 2002, Monsanto, a US multinational got the go-ahead from central regulators to sell its patented Bt cotton seed in India. The approval process was prolonged not only because it was the first of its kind, but also due to opposition from environmental groups, some of them reflexively opposed to anything American and others who believed that nature should not be artificially tampered with. But farmers, who had long suffered losses due to pest attacks on cotton crop, were in no mood to wait. About half of the country's load of pesticides used to be trained on cotton plants. To shave costs, farmers bought cheaper sprays, often spurious and ineffective, inflicting losses on themselves.

By the time Bt cotton neared the end of its eight-year regulatory approval grind, farmers were straining to get them hands on it. They were obliged by Ahmedabad's Navbharat Seeds, a company set up by a scientist, regarded variously as a do-gooder or an intellectual-property pirate. Farmers from not only Gujarat, but as far as Punjab and Andhra Pradesh snapped up the unapproved seeds. The regulator ordered the unauthorized crop to be destroyed but Modi's government pleaded helplessness. It had a vested interest in allowing competition to Monsanto's seed which was selling at Rs 1,650 a packet. And it imposed a price ceiling as well. The sale of fake seeds was a danger, but the presence of many players ensured that prices fell to Rs 450 a packet.

The worldwide agreement on textile and clothing in the middle of the last decade could not have been better timed. The abolition on textile import quotas by the United States and Europe resulted in a spurt in Chinese production — and demand for Indian cotton. From being a net importer India is now the second largest producer and exporter of cotton. Gujarat leads. Its productivity has risen from 226 kgs a hectare to 587 kgs a hectare in the past twelve years. Area under cotton has more than doubled from 6.6 lakh hectares to 14.2 lakh hectares. This was a repeat of the situation in the 1870s, when frequent crop failures in China flattered the fortunes of Gujarat's traders and laid the base for its industrialization.

In October 2013, I had occasion to see first-hand that when politics and ideology influence scientific decisions, people scorn regulators and take autonomous actions that can have grave consequences.

While the Supreme Court-appointed committee of scientists had sought an indefinite pause on field trials of genetically-modified crops, farmers in Vidarbha had sown cotton which is resistant to a weed-killing chemical even before regulators have approved its commercial release. After three years of safety trials, the US multinational Monsanto's Indian affiliate had applied in March 2013 for a license to sell its herbicide–resistant GM seed. But the Genetic Engineering Appraisal Committee did not consider the application in its meeting that month.

I saw the herbicide in action in the field of a well-to-do-farmer in Yavatmal. Weeds in the sprayed fields were wilting while cotton plants swayed in photosynthetic glee at the plight of their tormentors. The farmer had sown six of fifty acres under cotton with the seed that, he said, had been smuggled in by Gujarat dealers from the United States and Argentina. At Rs 800 per acre-covering packet of 650 grams, this is Rs 543 cheaper than legally saleable Bt cottonseed without weed-burning traits. Apart from two genes toxic to boll weevils, the herbicide-resistant version is spiked with another agro-bacterium gene which is immune to glyphosate, a widely used weed killer.

The stealth action of the farmers shows their yearning for labour-saving and profit-enhancing technologies, but is fraught with risk. Though GM crops are believed to be safe, protocols have to be observed to ensure they remain so. 'If the government does not give permission for new technology, we must adopt it by stealth or agitation to send a message,' said the farmer who asked not to be named or identified. According to him, 60,000 packets, enough to cover about as many acres, had been sold in Hinghanghat, Warora, Wani and Rajura taluks of Maharashtra's Wardha, Chandrapur and Yavatmal districts. He had used them first in 2012. I do not have evidence that Gujarat's farmers have adopted the technology; but I am sure its seed dealers would have first met home demand before turning elsewhere.

In conclusion, it can be said that Gujarat's agriculture is vibrant. It makes Gujarat's growth pro-poor. This is the result of an elegant combination of people's enterprise greased by government policies and complemented by corporate or cooperative action. When the waters of the Narmada spread further within a couple of years, Gujarat's agriculture could begin another winning run.

4. Resetting Tribal Lives

'Dignity, not dependency,' is Gujarat's mantra for uplifting tribals through high-yielding agriculture, dairying and skill development. It has not achieved its high ambition fully but those are issues that can be addressed with a problem-solving attitude.

When Shugriben Ratva bakes yellow maize *rotis* on a clay griddle over a roaring wood fire a tradition goes up in smoke. 'It is true that *rotis* made of yellow maize are sweeter than the traditional variety,' she says flipping the *roti*, which she has rolled between the folds of a polythene sheet. 'The yield is better and the rates are good. So we grow for the market, after retaining some for food,' she says justifying the victory of wallet over palate[1].

White *desi* maize has been the staple of Gujarati tribals. They find it tastier. But yellow hybrids are more productive and also in industrial demand because of higher starch content. So when Ratva sowed Sriram Bioseeds' hybrid maize, not only did the calculus of commerce enter her soot-blacked house in Chhota Udaipur, off Baroda, she made a cultural crossover as well.

Shifting tribal farmers from low-yield, low income maize to more productive agriculture has been at the heart of Gujarat's plan for tribal uplift. The formula is not radical; it was the template

---

[1] This story was published on 20 September 2013 in *Forbes India*.

of the 1960s Green Revolution in the plains. The novelty is in its application to poorly irrigated hilly tribal areas where farms are stamp-size, the weather erratic and the soil miserly.

Modi's model of development differs in its attitude to poverty removal. Modi does not believe in doles; he thinks the state must create conditions for people to help themselves. 'Give me power so I can empower you,' he remarked at a public rally. When *melas* were held in villages to inaugurate the separation of feeders for homes and farm pumps under Jyotigram, the government's publicity officers would tell people that the enhanced availability of electricity should be used for economic activity and not to watch more television. 'We said it was a technological aid to the potter and the *dhobi*,' Modi said.[2]

Modi's approach differs from the Tamil Nadu model with its tradition of direct income support by the state through the universal provision of subsidized cereals, pulses and edible oil, cooked food in schools and, under chief minister J Jayalalithaa, public canteens. The state's societal set up, shaped by Dravidian empowerment movements is such that there is a low tolerance for deficiency in public services; its political leadership and the bureaucracy are sensitive to this urge. Tamil Nadu has the finest public healthcare system in the country and its panchayati institutions work despite governments reputed for corruption. For these reasons, Tamil Nadu ranks high on social indicators. The economist Pranab Bardhan's remark that the Chinese make better capitalists now because they were better socialists then is apt for Tamil Nadu. But societies are not alike; Modi has patterned his style on Gujarat's ethos.

In 2006, Modi backed an officer, Anand Mohan Tiwari, who had innovative ideas for tribal welfare. Tiwari was an earnest and entrepreneurial officer. The posting to the tribal development department was not a coveted one, but Tiwari infused it with zeal.

---

[2] Speech at an exhibition of Muslim businesses on the banks of the Sarbarmati river in Ahmedabad on 7 February, 2014.

Tribals constitute 7.5 percent of Gujarat's population. While they are better off than tribals in the neighbouring states, within Gujarat they are the most deprived. A study by Amita Shah of the Gujarat Institute of Development Research showed that though more of them owned farms, albeit small, they spent less than other Gujaratis on food, education and health. During the ten years to the middle of the last decade, poverty among them actually increased while it declined in rural Gujarat.

Spending on tribal welfare has not been wanting. Since 1974, under what is known as tribal sub-plan, the slice of state budget outlays for welfare of tribals has to match their share of the population. Since the 1990s, tribal civic bodies in Gujarat have been getting larger parts of lard for small infrastructures like culverts. With none of this making a dent, Gujarati tribals had low expectations of the government. Tiwari found that his department did not have high ambition for them either. Science colleges for tribals were not considered a necessity. Providing running water connections was regarded as impractical, despite Himachal Pradesh showing the way. Green Revolution technologies had bypassed the tribals, while the dams that submerged their habitats were watering high-yielding crops in the plains. The tribal was supposed to settle for less.

For the Gujarati tribal to catch up with the rest, they had to break from poverty, caused primarily by low incomes from low-yielding agriculture. So a principal aspect of Gujarat chief minister's five-year, ten-point programme for their uplift, called Van Bandhu Kalyan Yojana, was income enhancement through a shift to high value vegetables; dairying; the acquisition of employable skills; and a hop from low-yielding *desi* maize, the staple, to smart hybrids.

But the switch was not easy as I discovered while studying this scheme with a fellowship from Delhi's Centre for Study of Development Societies. Tribals produce their own *desi* seed. Hybrid seeds have to be bought, are costly and a recurring seasonal expense as they cannot be reused. Private hybrid seed companies did not have the distribution web, while state-owned ones could not supply the required quantities. Hybrids need high doses of fertilizer, which was seldom available when most needed. Farmers, mostly illiterate, had to be coached in practices like spacing of plants for smart hybrids to deliver on their potential. High-cost hybrid agriculture dependent on unreliable monsoon can ruin farmers. There was also a cultural barrier to cross: tribals prefer the taste of white *desi* to industrial use starch-rich yellow hybrids.

To work up the enthusiasm of officials, the tribal department set income doubling in five years as its goal. For that the hybrid habit had to rapidly spread. It could not be business as usual. Rather than bank on the *babu's* rhythm, Tiwari decided to tap into the profit motive of private enterprises. 'If private sector can create wealth in non-tribal areas why to ignore them in tribal areas,' Tiwari reckoned.

Gujarat believes in public private partnerships. In the 1990s, under Chimanbhai Patel, the state's maritime board encouraged entrepreneurs like Nikhil Gandhi to set up private ports (Pipavav). To overcome the shortage of gynaecologists and obstetricians in state hospitals, Modi's government roped in private ones under the Chiranjeevi Yojana programme. The public sector Gujarat Green Revolution Company has pushed water-saving drips and sprinklers through private companies like Jain Irrigation and Plastro.

Tiwari had been persuaded by the American multinational Monsanto, whose genetically-modified Bt cotton approved for commercial use in 2002 now covers 93 percent of the crop's area and has made India the second largest producer (and exporter). There has been a maize revolution in the past decade triggered by hybrids released by private seed companies as well as government research institutes. Yearly production has increased by 66 percent to twenty million tons, and productivity is up 33 percent. Monsanto is a key player. To get Gujarat's tribals to join in, it provided 15,000 of them with seed, fertilizer and agronomic coaching free of cost in 2006, in a first of its kind experiment in the country. The tribal department supported that pilot called Project Rainbow; a doubling of yield encouraged it to scale up.

Under the successor Project Sunshine, the government decided to lubricate the entry of seed companies by providing eight kg of smart maize seed and 150 kg of fertilizer to every below-poverty-line tribal, enough to cover an acre each. The package, costing Rs 2,600 was sold at a deep discount, not given free. Farmers paid a graded fee, starting with Rs 500 in 2008 and Rs 1,100 in 2013. Eventually the subsidy would be abolished. By then there would be enough tribal converts to pull in the seed companies in. Apart from United Phosphorous and Shriram Bioseeds, American multinationals Pioneer Hi-bred International (a Dupont subsidiary) and Monsanto qualified.

The profit motive of private seed companies was to be the driving force. The government would open up a virgin market for them on the understanding that they would roll out their distribution networks once the threshold of demand for smart seeds was crossed. But environmentalists and the xenophobic RSS-affiliated farmers' union, the Bharatiya Kisan Sangh, were deeply suspicious. They feared (correctly) that getting tribal acceptance for yellow hybrids was a prelude to pushing genetically-modified maize. But there is no evidence that GM crops pose a threat to human health. GM maize was introduced in the US in 1997. Now it makes for eighty percent of the crop there.

'Our logic was that we do not care who doubles out income, whether it is MNCs or an American company or an Indian company as long as our objectives and goal are achieved,' Tiwari said, lounging on the spacious lawns of his house in Bharuch.[3] 'In that process we

---
[3] Tiwari was head of Gujarat State Ferilizer Corporation at the time of the interview.

used to issue public tenders; there was a rigorous selection process and if MNCs get the tender, so be it, we did not have any value judgment.'

Another piece of fresh thinking was the involvement of non-government organizations with proven record of rural service like Sadguru Foundation, to distribute seeds and fertilizer and also coach the tribals in the discipline of hybrids crops, bypassing the state's stretched agriculture extension system. Do-gooding industrial wives like Shruti Shroff were roped in, believing that they would be interested in earning goodwill than pecuniary benefit. A study by the Gujarat Institute of Development Research (GIDR) vindicated this faith, as almost all tribals officially certified as poor got their full entitlement of seed and fertilizer — in time. This was no small achievement considering the rampant corruption in government welfare schemes across the country. A few tribals complained of having to wait two-three days at the taluka distribution centres, but those were small gripes.

A third innovation was the creation of a compact group of professionals who were hired for the duration of Van Bandhu's various projects. Called Development Support Agency of Gujarat or D-SAG, it had to pull in funds scattered in various tribal schemes, cut through the compartmentalized activities of government agencies, and drive the progress of core projects.

The gleam in Premsinghbhai Ratva's eye when he confessed to earning about one lakh rupees — perhaps a first time event — from four acres of hybrid maize grown over one summer season, attested to the soundness of Gujarat's tribal uplift plan. A former *sarpanch* of Pilpur village in Chhota Udaipur, he said the shift from *desi* meant a switch from growing for subsistence to producing for the market. He claimed a yield of thirty quintals an acre, compared to the average of eight quintals in these parts. 'There is *fayda* in yellow maize,' he asserted.

It was an experience which Vithalbhai Jemta endorsed. He drives to towns if hybrid seeds are not available in the village. Jemta impresses with his knowledge of plant spacing and fertilizer application. The cost-benefit trade off however eluded Bapubhai Silot of Dahod's Bambori village. Owning a tractor, a mobike and a large house, he hardly seemed poverty stricken and eligible for subsidized seeds. But such transgressions must be overlooked as adoption of hybrid agriculture by elders like him can have a beneficial demonstration effect on those lower down in the village hierarchy. When government supplies arrived late last season, he plumped for *desi*. 'Yellow is good,' he said, 'but we must get the seed before *Chomasa* (June),' hinting that farmers like him were unlikely to buy seed from the market, if the government stopped subsidized sales.

But Milapsinh Padwal, a seeds retailer in Dahod's main bazaar said demand for hybrid seeds was rising. Instead of damaging his business as feared, the government's subsidized seeds programme had boosted it. In 2012, he sold twelve tons of hybrid seed in just two months, enough to cover over 800 acres, when government supplies arrived late.

Evaluation studies endorse anecdotal evidence of yield increases. Surveys by Anand University and GIDR show that hybrids have doubled the yield but savings have not kept pace because of the higher input costs. If tribals are to gain from smart agriculture, the government must push high-yield, low input seeds. So it must encourage research, including genetic modification, in seeds that are resilient to drought and salinity. Private companies can help by lowering the price of seed and rolling out their distribution network. They owe it to a government for lubricating their entry into a tough market. They are not making enough noise either. Prakashbai Ditabhai, a post-graduate non-tribal school-teacher farmer was unaware of hybrid maize, (though his tribal neighbour was growing it!) till he sought advice from a relative. Even then, he did not follow the farming protocol. Luckily he got a good yield. Monsanto said subsidies must end before demand emerges. It should instead take the lead in creating demand by licensing distributors.

Tribal farmers should be wedded to profit, not to any crop. GIDR says cotton and potato leave more on the table. An Amul-type cooperative, processing companies engaged in contract farming, or even a state-funded special purpose company programmed to wind up upon achieving the desired outcomes within a set period of time can take the logic of Gujarat's innovative approach to tribal welfare forward. This will be less fiscally-straining than a rights-based approach to poverty alleviation, which tugs eternally at the udders of the state.

∼

Tugging at the udders of cows instead was a bunch of women in Valsad's Amdha village. Most of them were Kokna Patels. A few belonged to PTGs or primitive tribal groups, though there was little in their demeanour to warrant that adjective. A dairy union brought them together. Half of the village's 240 households were members; fifty were active. In 2012, they supplied 77,000 litres of milk and earned nearly Rs 15 lakh, or nearly Rs 30,000 per supplier, on average.

That was enough cash to grease life between harvests. Dung-eating earthworms in woven plastic bags produced compost and more loose change. The women were wage labourers until 2004, when they hit upon dairying to escape the grind. Sarikabehn, wife of the dairy union's secretary, bought a heifer and reared it into a cow. She was one of the initiators.

Van Bandhu's dairy programme strives to pull tribal farmers from poverty by providing them cattle and support like training, collection centres, bulk chillers, milk testers, artificial inseminators, stainless steel containers and somatic cell counters (to check for infection). In the first phase lasting over seven years, 78,000 tribal families were to be converted to dairying at a cost of Rs 700 cr to be jointly shared by the state government, partner dairies and the tribals themselves. Four animals per household make the business viable. To cap subsidies, the government provides a household with two cows at discounted rates and cheap bank loans. It expects breeding to bring in the rest.

Elaborate measures have been instituted to ease the tribals' transition to dairying. Cattle suppliers have to bid to qualify. Camps put sellers and buyers together on specific days for match-making. Procurement committees assisted by vets are supposed to assure that animals sold can pay for themselves and they are not duds. Buyers can milk cattle at the camps at various intervals during the day to assure themselves of milk yield. Yet, tribals get shortchanged.

An early evaluation of the program revealed wide gaps between promise and performance. Reported yields fell by a third or a quarter between time of purchase and point of survey. Satisfaction levels had dropped. Cattle with multiple calves had been distributed, when they should not have been. Procurement officials typically downplayed the complaints; they blamed Gujarat's thriving dairy industry and rising demand for cows responsible for declining quality. Surveyors found that ineligible non-poor were claiming benefits.

Arti Thakar, the official who was overall in charge of dairying at Van Bandhu, said the programme was *'bilkul kamyab,'* (very successful). Official brochures endorsed the claim with facts. They cited the same agency — GIDR — that did the first evaluation, as finding a 'high level of satisfaction' in the subsequent round. Dairying had become the mainstay for half the participating families; in Sabarkantha the proportion was as high as 78 percent, was the official lore. In some talukas average milk yield was reported to have risen by 35 to 40 percent. Concerns were also flagged off: scanty rainfall, lack of fodder, shortage of good cattle, unaffordable feed, and a legacy of inferior animals that should be culled to save fodder but were not owing to religious sensitivities.

These are perhaps the unavoidable hazards of any scheme that aims at the mass conversion of down-and-out tribals to dairying. It is not a factory process where you feed inputs at one end and get milk at the other, said Surendrabahadur Singh of Vasudhara Dairy.

A resident of Uttar Pradesh, who has been initiating tribals into dairying for thirty years, Singh found no tradition of dairying among tribals when he took up the job. 'They would drink black tea.' Experts at the National Dairy Development Board had pronounced Valsad Dairy a non-starter for this reason. But its trustees persevered. They wanted to give the tribals an alternative to toiling in the cities. From 2,000 litres of milk a day to 3.80 lakh, the dairy has come a long way. The membership has risen to 1.17 lakh; 64 percent of them are tribal.

Vasudhara Dairy is the kind of cooperative that is fully aligned with Van Bandhu's ambition because it understands tribals and inspires trust in them. This cannot be said of many of the other dairies, which Van Bandhu has perforce to partner with for want of an option. Some of these are run by politicians who are less than public-minded.

If Vasudhara Dairy had its way Van Bandhu's focus on the most poor tribals would be amended. Those below the poverty line have little income and no land. Wage labour leaves scant time for the kind of care that hybrid cattle need: green fodder, nutritious feed, copious water and space for a shed. There are bio-rhythms to be observed like signs of heat in cattle, the time for insemination and the daily milking schedule which is governed by hormones. Singh thinks any tribal who has the inclination must be given the dole to get started. There is little harm done even if the non-poor get it. In fact, they might inspire by example. For him aspiration was the key to the success of dairying, followed by training, acquisition of cattle, heifer rearing and pregnant cow care. 'We tell people to be business-minded, not to be subsidy-oriented,' he says.

Politicians may count success by the numbers of cattle distributed or amount of loan disbursed. But dairying is a slow, accretive process. It demands a discipline many tribals are not prepared for. Jobs in Gujarat's many industrial hubs are a big attraction. But they do not reckon with the collateral damage: hazardous work conditions, precarious life in slums and the neglect of schooling.

~

The vocational training centre at Vaghaldhara in Valsad prepares tribal youth for industrial jobs. It was set up by a senior advocate who had made it big in Surat and wanted to give back to the community he was born into. It is love's labour. The exposed red brick building with airy rooms and cool kota stone flooring was designed by founder, Ishwer J Desai's architect daughter herself. There were 282 students when I visited. They were distributed across eight courses, some of them three-years long, others of six months duration, designed with German assistance. It was a residential co-ed facility. The students slept on bunk beds and meals — frugal — were free.

Desai responded to the government's call for partnership believing if he did not step forward, bad coins would, defeating the government's purpose because 'the current national crisis is a crisis of character.' He is right because the tribal department had previously engaged such suspicious-sounding entities as Bajrang Vyayamashala for computer education. Desai contributed land as a third of the investment; the government pitched in with the remaining Rs 5 crore, which it disbursed in less than two years, to Desai's surprise. It has a target of training 3,000 students over five years. In just two years Desai said 800 had done the drill, with nearly 90 percent success in getting jobs.

Van Bandhu's vocational training scheme has gone through many changes, a testimony to the problem-solving attitude of the leadership of the tribal affairs department under Tiwari. Initially it enlisted government supported institutes like Cipet (plastic technology) and the Indo-German Tool Room. But their intake was in the low hundreds. Some well-known private computer training companies and industry chambers were roped in next. They did not live up to their reputations. The third crop of trainers was selected for their technical competence. Courses and fees payable to them (by the government) were standardized. 'Village-based training,' at doorsteps was abandoned for residential training centres, to draw tribal youth out of their family comfort zones, and prepare them for life in cities.

Kinjol Gamit of Tapi district was training to be a daughtsperson at Vaghaldahara. Her father, who serves income tax notices, suggested the course on the advice of his friend. Ankit Chaudhari, also of Tapi, loves to fix things and was training to be an electrician. His father's job is to hook up homes with wire for a cable TV operator. Mahesh Kakad of Dharampur in Valsad wanted to be a welder, and self-employed.

This was perhaps their first prolonged stay away from homes.

In Dahod, the training centre was run by Gramin Vikas Trust. It provided certificate courses in plumbing and masonry from rented premises. Seventy students were supposed to be present, but only a few were seen during the visit. Technical Adviser A K Jain, said the students were much in demand from the construction industry because the courses not only taught the 'how' of a job, but also the 'why' (of say, mixing cement and sand in a particular ratio). A certificate from the centre could inflate wages 100 percent. But the courses needed to evolve because construction practices were changing. The use of pre-fabricated panels, ready-mix concrete, composite aluminum wall claddings and tower lifts to hoist material demanded skills that the centre was eager to provide, if builders were willing to pitch in.

But there was a catch. The Vaghaldara institute was going through pangs of anxiety over its future. A shake up in the tribal affairs department had impeded the flow of grants. 'In the last one year, the government did not fill the post of secretary in a regular way,' says Desai.[4] 'There used to be people who were given additional charge of the (tribal) department. So the other responsibilities become important and we feel sometimes that we are left in the lurch.' If the government continued to be erratic in funding, the Vaghaldhara centre would have to charge fees. Tribal students would lose out.

'Tough time for genuine and reputed rural development NGOs,' wrote Harnath Jagawat in the 2012 annual report of the Sadguru Foundation. The secretary who replaced Tiwari tried to go back to the old ways of getting things done departmentally. He later resigned and won on a BJP ticket from a reserved Assembly constituency in Ahmedabad. The surprise was that Modi allowed the scheme to sag for two years before correcting course with a secretary aligned to Van Bandhu's core philosophy.

---

[4] When interviewed in April 2013.

5. CHINESE-STYLE IMPLEMENTATION

The combination of Hindu cultural nationalism and economic development makes Gujarat's model Chinese in characteristics. Modi's capacity for audacious implementation and his impatience with democratic checks and balances belong in a Dragon state.

'So many things work in Gujarat that it hardly feels like India,' gushed the *Economist* in a 2011 report, headlined 'India's Guangdong'.[1] Gujarat, with its strong, China-like share of manufacturing could be a model for India, which has difficulty absorbing rural labour. It quoted a ranking of Indian states by management consultancy McKinsey and the role Gujarat might play as India's industrial locomotive.

China is the workshop of the world. Gujarat vies for that position within India. Manufacturing contributes a fourth of its GDP, against a sixth nationally. The proportion rises to China's level when the value created by the construction industry, and water, gas and electricity utilities are added. Like China's Gujarat's industrial growth has ridden on its infrastructures and quiescent labour. Ten of its forty-one ports are navigable in all weather conditions. A gas grid of 2,800 km serves the power, ceramic and glassware industries.[2] Gujarat has a dense network of fine roads. It has more power than it

---
[1] India's Guangdong, *Economist*, 7 June, 2011.
[2] Vibrant Gujarat 2013 presentation.

can use. A third of the Delhi-Mumbai industrial corridor running along a freight-only rail line which is under construction will be in Gujarat. About half-a-dozen vast industrial estates, Chinese in scale, are proposed.

Modi raves about the ease of doing business in Gujarat; it usually tops the rankings. He also boasts about 'zero-level man-days' loss. This is not quite true. In May 2011, workers at the General Motors car plant struck work for fifty days. They were protesting against health hazards, the transfer of workers to dealerships and the management's reluctance to make a long-term wage deal. Since then there have been strikes at the Bombardier factory, Arvind textile mills, and Larsen & Toubro's heavy engineering plants. But strikes and lockouts have diminished in number and intensity across the country since the 1980s. Despite recent incidents Gujarat remains an oasis of industrial peace. The incidents of unrest have declined from forty-two in 2003 to twenty-eight in 2011. The numbers of man-days lost at 36,000 is a third of the decade-ago number. Fewer workers tends to be involved.[3] Trade unions are less likely to be confrontational in Gujarat; they are known for the art of compromise unlike their peers, say in Haryana or Tamil Nadu. China's labour flexibility is often cited as a reason for manufacturing growth. Gujarat has amended the restrictive Industrial Disputes Act to allow workers in units employed in special economic zones to be laid off with one month notice on payment of a higher compensation. It allows units in SEZs to be closed down with two months notice. 'Fixed term employment' is also possible. Because of this investment bank Goldman Sachs said in a March 2014 report that Gujarat's manufacturing employment rose 60 percent between 2000 and 2012, against 22 percent in West Bengal.

---

[3] Gujarat Socio-economic surveys. Strikes and lockouts were forty-two in 2003, twelve in 2008 and twenty-eight in 2011. The number of workers involved declined from 7,973 in 2003 and 8,215 in 2006 to 2,966 in 2010. The mandays lost dropped from 1,22,098 in 2003 to 35,873 in 2011.

Getting rich was glorious in Gujarat long before Chinese liberalizer Deng Xiaoping's exhortation to his countrymen in 1992. Only a Gujarati chief minister could pay tribute to India's ascetic founding father by inaugurating Gandhinagar's new conference venue called Mahatma Mandir with a celebration of wealth creators.[4] Modi is a liberalizer unlike RSS ideologues who are not enamoured of foreign investment. When attacked for privatizing ports, Modi remarked that 'the people of Gujarat are enterprising and they want minimum government.'[5] Like 'One-Chop Zhu' (Rongji), the mayor who presided over the development of Shanghai's Pudong financial district, Modi is a slasher of red-tape. Pollution control board consents are given electronically, there is a facility for provisional consents and the online tracking mechanism is transparent says industry club, FICCI. The land records are computerized, land use information is available on a website, and data along sixty-five attributes is provided.[6] Units covered by labour laws are allowed to self-certify their compliance with safety regulations.[7] Lift inspections have been outsourced to private parties.

Port-led development has become something of a mantra with the Gujarat government. It has got a boost under Modi. Gujarat established the country's first private port at Pipapav in 1992. There was no policy or precedent for such an initiative at that time. It is now owned by APM Terminals, one of the largest container terminal operators in the world. Speaking at a conference of chief ministers in Delhi in 2006, Modi demanded that port-based development should be incorporated in the national economic strategy.

Peninsular India lost much of its economic advantage when the country turned insular after Independence. Kandla port was

---

[4] The fifth Vibrant Gujarat Investment Meet held on 12 January, 2011.
[5] Aditi Phadnis, *Political Profiles of Cabals and Kings*, Business Standard, 2009.
[6] FICCI and Bain & Company's booklet, *Empowering India: Better G2B Relations*.
[7] This, according to Prof Indira Hirway in EPW of 28 May, 2011, was allowed by Government of India in December 2003.

developed to make up for the loss of Karachi to Pakistan after Partition. But the rail link connecting it was narrower than the standard national track, which meant a break in journey for goods headed to the port. Road connectivity was poor. It was symbolic of the country's apathy to trade.

Sea trade has underpinned Gujarat's prosperity down the ages. It therefore woke up to the opportunity loss much before the other states did. Realizing that there was no Constitutional bar on developing the so-called 'minor' ports that were within state jurisdiction, it set up the country's first maritime board in 1982. A decade later, it articulated a policy of developing ten 'world class' ports, six of them privately, and four with the government as a minority partner. This coincided with the country's reforms and openness to external trade. In 2004-05, the minor port of Sikka overtook the major port of Vishakapatnam as the country's biggest port. It is the country's largest oil handling port serving its biggest refinery. Minor ports are now less inappropriately called non-major ports! Gujarat's port policies have passed the test of investor approval. Maersk, Shell, Reliance, Adani and Essar are some of the port operators in the state. Its ports handle a fifth of India's sea traffic.

Kutch is a Shenzen-like metaphor for port-led development in India. It was in Shenzen that China made a break with the past and experimented with controlled capitalism (called Socialism with Chinese Characteristics). A fishing village of just three square kilometers and 30,000 people, it became China's first special economic zone in 1980 because of its proximity to Hong Kong. Foreign investors were allowed to make shoes, toys and electronics for exports. Today it has a population of twelve million, half of them migrants. Despite being one of the richest cities, it grew at 10.5 percent in 2013. And it has moved from labour-intensive industries to knowledge-intensive biotechnology, information technology, new energy, new material and the creative industries.

The Gujarat and central governments lavished attention and money on Kutch for its economic reconstruction when an earthquake devastated it in 2001. These efforts are detailed in the first chapter. Gautam Adani's port and special economic zone at Mundra carried that logic forward. Together they have transformed Kutch from an arid backwater which people were fleeing to a place where people flock. In the past decade, its population, albeit sparse, has increased by 32 percent, the second fastest after dense Surat.

Mundra was a fishing village when Gautam Adani began constructing a port there in 1998. As a commodities trader, he made quick profits but realized that the business was not backed by assets and had little purchase with investors. The shift to developing infrastructure — ports, power, industrial enclaves, and gas distribution — meant a mental switch to making patients profits over time.

The shift in strategy was the result of business opportunism. An official in India's Secretariat for Industrial Approvals says a US commodities multinational, forced to abandon its salt works in the United States for environmental reasons, found an attractive alternative in the saline expanses of the Rann of Kutch. Since Adani was reputed to be close to chief minister Chimanbhai Patel, it engaged him to acquire a large swathe of salt pan. Adani agreed but got the land registered in his name and proposed a partnership. The US multinational, a wholly-family owned enterprise, did not agree. When it walked away Adani was left with a lot of saline land and a jetty. Upon the advice of a far-sighted dentist friend, Adani decided it could be an alternative to the inefficient government-owned Kandla port and a gateway to the North Indian hinterland.

In Gujarat port policy, Adani found the perfect fit for his plan. He partnered with the government, but later took the port entirely

---

[8] Company's annual report 2013.

private. When a commerce minister, impressed by a visit to China, announced a special economic policy for India in 2000, Adani was ready and waiting. At 6,500 acres, his is the largest notified SEZ in the country with exports of over Rs 7,300 cr.[8] But it is facing regulatory troubles, over violation of environmental norms.

Adani is one of a handful of Gujarat 'princelings'. That is what he could be called if he were in China. It is a term that refers to the children of Communist Party leaders who have set up thriving businesses by leveraging their proximity to power. Adani is known to be close to Modi. He was part of the Resurgent Group of Gujarat that stood by Modi after the 2002 riots. In 2013, Adani's group withdrew sponsorship for Wharton India Economic Forum after the business school cancelled Modi's speech by videoconference (the United States had denied him a visa), following protests from professors and students.[9]

Under Modi's watch, the Adani group's annual turnover has swelled from Rs 3,000 cr ($0.69 billlion)[10] to Rs 54,000 cr ($8.7 billion)[11] an eighteen-fold rise over thirteen years. Adani admits that his group has grown 'exponentially'. 'We never thought we would be so big in 1995,' he said in a conversation. From vast tracts of cheap land, to choice cities for gas distribution to quick clearances, the Adani group has had a charmed existence over the past decade. But Adani's growth is debt fuelled, like that of most infrastructure groups. The port makes money, but the power business is bleeding, as the expected coal mine leases from the Gujarat government did not materialize reportedly because of a misalignment between political intention and bureaucratic action. This has necessitated imports from Indonesia, whose government has imposed a minimum export

---

[9] *The Hindu*, 4 March, 2013.
[10] M Rajshekhar, *Economic Times* 5 Sept, 2013. Exchange rate Rs 43 to the dollar, according to Economic Survey.
[11] Website says turnover was $8.7 billion in 2013. Since founding the group's business has grown 'exponentially' the chairman's message on the website on 4 March 2014 said.

price on coal. While the power business has received regulatory relief, it is not clear whether the group can service its debts without becoming asset light. It is among India's top debtors to banks. But Adani's personal fortune has climbed up from $1.8 billion in 2009 to $2.8 billion in 2013, though his rank in the Forbes list of billionaires has fallen from 397 to 609 during this period.

Adani is not an exception. Rare is the infrastructure group that can succeed without government support. The tidal waves of Telugu entrepreneurship, for instance, washing over airports at Mumbai, Delhi and Hyderabad, the metro rail projects in Delhi and Bangalore, the coal-fired power plants, the ports, the highways, dams and malls have gained velocity from chief minister Y S Rajshekar Reddy's 'Andhra model of development,' and obliging ministers in charge of the national infrastructure ministries.

Modi says he is a 'trustee' of the people, but a former Gujarat bureaucrat who turned around ailing state companies has a different take. 'He is not corrupt in the sense that he is not after money,' says Alexander Luke. 'Nobody can influence him. But he will give away public wealth to cronies who do his bidding, or project him.'

Pranab Bardhan, Professor of economics at the University of California in Berkeley told the *Indian Express* about Gujarat: 'I saw data that the total amount of subsidies to the corporate sector, especially in the form of tax concessions and capital subsidies, was ten times what was spent on agriculture and food subsidies.'[12]

The spin that Modi's officials put on corporate subsidies and concessions is that they are investments that will more than pay back the state over time. Corporate leaders say Modi's style of harvesting campaign finance through a few industrial groups is preferable to spreading the 'levy' across industries. Crony wealth, they assert, is due to favours bestowed alright, but is multiplied in large measure

---

[12] *Indian Express*, interview with Yamini Lohia, 5 March, 2014.

by enterprise and propensity for risk. When we entered Mundra in 2005 (for the SEZ) land was selling for Rs 5,000 an acre, Gautam Adani said. Six years later, the asking rate was Rs 25 lakh.

China, post liberalization in 1978, has seen humungous corruption. Cronyism has grown like bamboo shoots in a spring rain. But China has also pulled the largest number of people in history out of poverty over a relatively short period of time. According to the World Bank its GDP at $8.2 trillion is more than four times India's $1.8 trillion though it was about the same when China changed economic course. China, they say, is condemned to grow, as the Communist Party can retain its monopoly on power only if people are not restive. So it is with Modi's Gujarat. The Hindutva fervour that keeps Modi in power will fizzle out without the fizz of development.

Like Modi's government, Gujarat's industrial favourites score high on execution. Anyone who visits Mundra port will be impressed. It can handle very large vessels. It is the country's second largest in terms of cargo moved. 'I want Mundra to be seen not as a private asset but as a national asset,' Adani says. The attached ultra-mega power plant is a marvel. Though coal-fired, the Italian marble floor housing the instrumentation panels gleams like that of a star hotel. The Reliance Jamnagar refinery is an ode to execution. It ranks high on a measure of complexity called the Nelson index, because of its ability to process a variety of sweet to sour crudes. The Essar's steel plant at Hazira is the largest single location facility for flat products.

Audacity is another hallmark of Modi's style. In January 2013, he inaugurated one of two 28-storeyed towers, and the first of more to come at Gujarat International Finance Tec-City or GIFT. The enclave, twelve kilometres from Ahmedabad airport was to become an international financial services centre, rivaling Mumbai. With an

---

[13] GIFT official website.

area of 3.5 square kilometers, and 8.5 million of sq feet of built up space, it was supposed to be bigger than London, Paris, New York and Pudong (Shanghai) financial districts.[13]

The project may become a monument to hubris and reminds one of China's many ghost cities. It was conceived in the middle of the last decade, before the global banking crisis. The Gujarat government partnered with IL&FS Limited, a pioneer in private development of infrastructures like toll bridges (Delhi-Noida); municipal water supply (Tamil Nadu's hosiery centre, Tirupur); and bypasses (Madhya Pradesh's Rau-Pithampur).

In those days when reformers were in a hurry to complete the integration of India with the global economy and capital account convertibility was seen as an unfinished agenda, Finance Minister P Chidambaram had got the Percy Mistry Committee to give a report on remaking Mumbai into an international financial services centre. The plan was bold in vision. It foresaw Mumbai 'not as an offshore appendix but as a metaphor for deregulating, liberalizing and globalizing all parts of the Indian financial system at a much faster rate.'

As a continental economy, India must become a producer and exporter of international financial services and capture an increasing share of the rapidly growing global international financial services market, the report said. To achieve this, its financial centre in Mumbai must compete with global financial centres in New York, London and Singapore, in two phases, by 2020.

Mumbai's champions said Indian clients had bought international financial services worth $13 billion in 2005. They estimated the purchases to rise to $48 billion, and even to $70 billion, if the economy grew annually at nine percent. India had the advantage of location; it could trade with Asia and Europe during daytime. India had human capital and mindshare, as Indians were employed in global financial services firms. A strong securities market and advanced trading platforms were seen as plus points.

But a lot had to be done before Mumbai could get there. First of all, India would have to follow stable and credible macro-economic policies. It would have to slash the fiscal deficit, both at the central and state levels, and pursue prudent fiscal policies. The public debt to GDP ratio would have to shrink. India would have to go capital convertible. Mumbai's infrastructure and governance would have to improve to attract international talent and permit world-class lifestyles. Law enforcement would have to be strict and there could be no laxity in security. The city should become tolerant to all communities and welcoming of migrants.

The project to make Mumbai an international financial centre could have been a metaphor for national purpose and determination. But leaders in Delhi and Mumbai were cold to it. The 2007 blueprint did not even get the courtesy of extensive debate.

This is where Modi stepped in. He hoped that Mumbai's financial community, fed up with its crumbling infrastructure, would make the switch, if Ahmedabad was connected with a high-speed rail link. But financial centres need to be ecosystems that make world class living possible. Ahmedabad just does not measure up. Without assurance on the macro-economic policies (outlined above) GIFT would remain more of a real estate play. Shailesh Pathak, an investment banker and construction equipment financier, who is familiar with the project sees GIFT city as a back office for financial services and information technology firms, like Bangalore and Hyderabad.

China, meanwhile, has bested India even on this score. In September 2012 it launched the Shanghai Free Trade Zone as a Hong Kong-like enclave on the mainland, where capital and commodities would flow freely. The Shanghai zone has the personal endorsement of Premier Li Keqiang, who wants it to be a crucible for bolder financial reforms.

The prettification of the Sabarmati also spells audacity. It is an example that Indian cities on riverbanks, like Delhi, could emulate. What used to be a dry riverbed, sewer and garbage dump is now a twenty-two-km stretch of channel, uniformly 275 metres wide, its waters coming from the Narmada canal and retained by a barrage. Concrete walls have been sunk fifty feet into the riverbed and rise above the highest flood-water level of the past 100 years. Sewage that used to pour into the river is now piped to treatment plants. The banks have been filled up and made level with hillocks of earth. About 202 hectares of prime land have been reclaimed; offices, hotels and posh apartments to be located on twenty-nine hectares will help recover the cost of Rs 1,150 cr, an official says, as we drive down a newly carved out arterial road, to a vast park. Once fully developed, the stretch will resemble Mumbai's Marine Drive.

The project was conceived by a French architect in 1965; work commenced towards the beginning of the last decade and gathered pace towards the end. Apart from recreation facilities, event grounds, exhibition venues and extensive greenery, a traditional Sunday scrap market with 1,200 vendors has been recreated. The *dhobi ghat* has been relocated to a 'laundry campus'. It has 200 cubicles, each with power and water connections for washing machines. About 10,000 families have been relocated and given new houses but they had to knock on the Gujarat High Court first.

Boosting the value of underlying land to pay for infrastructures developed on it, is a Chinese trick that has been employed by the Ahmedabad municipal corporation for Sabarmati. Chinese provincial governments have expenditure obligations that are vastly in excess of their income. The need to raise revenue explains the infrastructure binge in China. Since land is owned by the state, eviction is easy. Between 1992 and 2005, twenty million Chinese farmers were reportedly evicted and 21 percent of arable land taken away for non-agricultural purposes. This has triggered massive protests. In India, land sale to pay for urban infrastructures is a novelty that is catching on.

Though Gujarat is rapidly urbanizing — 43 percent population-wise — protests from farmers against land acquisition have been relatively muted. A law that restricted sale of farm land only to those who lived within an eight-km radius was relaxed in drought-hit areas by the Congress government in 1987. The BJP government abolished this rule in 1995. It also allowed farmland up to ten hectares to be converted to non-agriculture use. The Modi government made further relaxations in 2003. Land allottees under tenancy and urban ceiling laws and those given wasteland could sell it after a holding period, and also use it for non-farming purposes.

Like the Chinese, Modi is keen on 'rurbanization' or providing urban comforts in rural areas, and creating new cities. About half a dozen investment regions are planned along ports, and the special freight rail line being laid between Delhi and Mumbai. Some of these will be truly Chinese in size, like the one at Dholera.

But a cooperative route to redevelopment is being tried out for new townships to reduce social conflict and upfront investment. Rather than dispossess owners, they are required to cede just as much land as is required for backbone facilities like roads, drains and sewerage. The enhanced value of land left behind more than compensates for the loss. Periodic revision of guideline prices brings them in line with market rates. The government is not averse to paying more; this is how it acquired 2,500 hectares in the last quarter of 2013, to beat a new national law that will make such purchases difficult and costly.[14]

Though Gujarat has not seen protests over land grabs like the ones in West Bengal and Maharashtra, simmering discontent sometimes

---

[14] According to Maheshwar Sahu, who was industries secretary till February 2014, 2,500 hectares was acquired by GIDC from September to December 2013, in Sanand, Dahej and Mehsana.

bursts forth. When I met him at Gandhinagar's MLA apartments in the first week of April 2011, Kanubhai Kalsaria was nursing sore feet that had crepe bandages wrapped around them. Nineteen days after leading a 300-km march from the coastal town of Mahuva to the state capital, his feet were still hurting. The protest was against a cement plant which detergent maker Karsanbhai Patel was setting up in his constituency. Kalsaria was angry that the project was conceived in secrecy. Though three-times MLA, he was not even informed about the project. 'Is there no obligation to take me into confidence?' he asked.

The industrialist putting up the plant was himself a giant-slayer. With his inexpensively-priced washing powder, he had taken on the mighty Hindustan Unilever, and forced the Anglo-Dutch consumer goods corporation to rethink its marketing and pricing strategies. Patel was a Modi supporter. He was among the business leaders who had formed the Resurgent Group of Gujarat. But now he was in the line of people's fire.

Kalsaria is a general surgeon who practices at a charitable trust hospital and performs cut-price surgical operations. He believes that politics like his medical practice must heal and not hurt. In that sense he was a misfit in a communal party with a sectarian agenda. Kalsaria was under pressure from the BJP to quit. But he would not resign asserting that he was answerable to the people. He was not expelled either because of local goodwill. Kalsaria was not opposed to development. He would have welcomed, say, a car factory. But a cement plant, in his view, would devastate seven villages. It would soak up water from a dam that he had helped erect to stop the ingress of sea water at high tide. Limestone mining to feed the cement factory would eat up fertile farm land. The plant would create a few hundred direct jobs but what would happen to the scores of onion dehydrating plants and cotton ginning units that between them employed 20,000 people?

Kalsaria said kangaroo public hearings had been conducted; consent from village elites had been obtained with offers of contracts, earthmoving equipment, and a temple building. Those who were adamant in their opposition had been intimidated.

The then industries secretary characterized the issue as an 'ego tussle'. The limestone mine was on wasteland. The cement company had assured that channels bringing rainwater to the reservoir would not be blocked; in fact more would be created. Overall, the project would benefit the people.

Kalsaria moved the Supreme Court against the plant; the Congress party at the centre, ever spoiling for a chance to needle Modi, told the court it had been misinformed about the project and had withdrawn environmental approval. The cement project is off. Kalsaria quit the BJP, contested on the platform of harmony, but lost badly.

Kalsaria's victory would have been an indictment of Modi's brand of development but his defeat should not been seen as a complete endorsement either, just as the defeat of Andhra chief minister Chandrababu Naidu in the 2004 elections cannot be regarded as a wholesale repudiation of his sensible economic policies. Kalsaria blames wrong strategy for it; not voter disapproval.

Modi is certainly deficient in the dissent department. Kalsaria was seeking reconsideration of an industrial project for the sake of people; he was not challenging the chief minister's authority. Modi could not see the difference.

The elimination of so-called terrorists in staged encounters by police henchmen (now in jail); the stiff opposition to appointment of an independent ombudsman (Lokayukta); the extensive surveillance; the subversion of the investigative and prosecution process to protect Hindu criminals involved in the 2002 riots; and the disdainful treatment of the political opposition makes one wonder whether Modi's comfort with democracy stops at elections — and well short of Constitutional checks and balances, reflecting the Chinese Communist Party's unease with Western-style separation of powers.

This may be one of the reasons that Modi likes China. He has made more than one visit to that country. Unlike the United States and the European Union, China does not lecture him on human rights. Given its own poor record in this area, it is open to doing business with all sorts of regimes, on the principle that what happens within a country's borders is its own concern. During the 2011 visit, the Chinese gave Modi an effusive welcome. Modi appreciatively noted that Chinese companies were keen to work in Gujarat. He offered to set up a Mandarin school. China's rise makes Modi wary but its combination of nationalism and economic heft is in sync with his own outlook.

It is a philosophy that grates on those who imagine India as a vibrant and compassionate society, not just a thriving economy hitched to notions of past grandeur. They see in Gujarat's dominant values a pale version of the Beijing Consensus, which the *Economist* described as 'going capitalist, staying autocratic.' For them Gujarat under Modi is an experiment in rewriting the India story in muscular Hindu nationalistic terms over Nehru's liberal, secular expression. Nilanjan Mukhopadhyay has observed presciently that Modi is India's first major political leader cast in an anti-Nehruvian mould.

6. Opportunistically Inclusivise

⁂

Can governance be good without justice? National ambition has made Modi reach out to the very community which he ignored for long years as chief minister. Will the seduction of power and the compulsions of electoral politics temper ingrained hard line beliefs?

'It does not matter which community you belong to, how you do *puja path*; what matters is how much hunger or aspiration you have. We have to link everyone in development.'

It was mid-morning. The sun had trained its full gaze at the audience on the banks of the Sabarmati River. The media had turned up in strength. There were more correspondents and cameramen than invitees. But Modi was unfazed. His 'Vision of growth for all Indians,' was addressed to the country's 160 million Muslims.

The occasion was the inauguration of an exhibition of Ahmedabad's Muslim businesses. The displays, if representative, were not a canvas of optimism. They advertised just how much Gujarat's economic progress had bypassed the community, despite its recovery after the 2002 riots. The participants were property developers, restaurateurs and car dealers (besides state government departments). The sole manufacturer-participant was a supplier of industrial valves. Despite being in existence since 1890, its annual turnover was very low; family divisions and a catastrophic arson attack during the riots had kept it stunted.

The factory was set up by the granddad of the organizer, Zafar Sareshwala, an Islamic banker, who suffered financial losses during the riots and planned to move with family to London. From being an opponent, Sareshwala has turned apologist for Modi. A dealership for expensive German cars acquired after the riots allows him to hawk the 'bygones are bygones let's move on' line. There are not many takers for it within his community. A sprinkling of Hindu businesses, car sellers mainly, at the exhibition gave token support to its theme, 'business harmony to grow together.' A property portal's unique selling proposition — a listing of two dozen apartment complexes in and around the city where Muslims were not barred from investing — was comment in itself on Gujarati society. The Gujarat Chambers of Commerce and Industry had declined to participate; it may have been a purely business decision, or even a measure of the communal distance.

As far as vision statements went, there was little to quibble in Modi's speech. He touched all the right cords. He noted that Muslims were in line with Gujarat's ethos; they were a self-made community that was especially thriving in districts like Kutch, where it has a significant presence. Did he not engage a research agency from Tamil Nadu in 2003 to streamline the making of kites (presumably a Muslim specialty)? Officials had tittered at his decision. But by studying the work flow, the agency had compressed thirty-four discrete processes into fourteen and an informal industry had grown from Rs 35 cr to Rs 700 cr in annual business. (It was Rs 500 cr while inaugurating the international kite festival in the city, two weeks before!)

Modi said he admired Muslim artistic talent and their felicity with fingers. He exhorted them to make the best of the state's skill development programme. Were not Muslims good at embroidery and stitching? And was not Gujarat a big producer of cotton? What a loss then, that India was exporting the stuff when it should be dressing up the world. He repeated his nostrum of the

5Fs for making India an exporter of branded apparel (Farm-Fibre-Fabric-Fashion-Foreign markets). China had made the most of the abolition of textile quotas on exports at the beginning of the last decade. India's labour laws and poor business climate had turned its garments business into commoditized job work; it was time to free up the animal spirits, create massive jobs, and retain more of the value addition. He held out the promise of gender parity for Muslim women and hoped some of them would become entrepreneurs. He had given them peace and security. Riots have not recurred.

'I find a big difference between BJP and Modi,' said Sareshwala. 'We feel we can trust him.' Sareshwala believes that the RSS has little influence on Modi. Modi had swatted leaders from the RSS and its affiliate the VHP, who had tried to upstage or under cut him. But there is little evidence that he has unsubscribed to its core, Hindu supremacist beliefs. 'Modi is good for the state, and we are part of the state,' Sareshwala says. 'There is no discrimination against Muslims.'

It is a statement that hides from facts. 'Modi has done little to engage with the community,' says Hanif Lakdawala, an Ahmedabad-based psychiatrist, who provides community health services to slum residents through an NGO. 'Muslims have not reconciled,' he adds. 'They have accepted that they are second-class citizens.' The communal divide that existed before the riots has become more pronounced. There is little exchange between communities. Achyut Yagnik endorses that observation. A former trade union leader, he has authored a book on Gujarat's communal history.

The unrelenting media focus on Modi's administration since the 2002 riots has prevented the recurrence of new ones. The Muslim underworld that thrived on bootlegging and derived legitimacy by acting as community protector has been decimated. The savage reprisals that followed the barbaric burning of Hindutva volunteers in a train at Godhra station in 2002, may have convinced Muslims that sublimating their anger was wiser than venting it.

The long stretch of peace, an aberration in Gujarat's recent history, pocked as it is with communal clashes has helped Muslims. Nearly 60 percent of them reside in urban areas and self-employment, like rickshaw driving or vehicle repairing, is the main occupation for half of those households.[1] Another 10 percent live on casual wages. These groups are affected the most when there are forced shutdowns. The Muslim share of steady income salaried employment is 10 percentage points less than of Hindus. In rural areas too, more than 80 percent are either self-employed or labourers.[2] Riots set the community back after every recovery.

∼

Modi protests that Muslims are doing better than in other states and this seems to be by and large true. The central government's Sachar Committee which inquired into the condition of Muslims across the country and gave its report in 2006, said they held 8.5 percent of higher posts in Gujarat's public sector undertakings and a tenth share of the Group A jobs. This was in line with their share of the population. In general category jobs, Muslim share was higher — 16 percent. In West Bengal, which has been always ruled by sympathetic governments, Muslims held just one percent of higher posts and six percent of general category jobs, off line with their quarter share of the population. Though Kerala gives Muslims more jobs, the share is not representative.

---

[1] The Sachar Committee quoting the 2001 Census says the share of urbanization among Gujarati Muslims was 58.7 percent, while the state as a whole was 37.4 percent urbanized.

[2] NSSO's latest large sample survey conducted between July 2009 and June 2010 and published in June 2013 says 49.2 percent of urban Muslim households in Gujarat cited self-employment as their main occupation. 10.8 percent said they were casual labourers. In rural areas, 43.6 percent of Muslim households were self-employed and 41.6 percent were daily workers.

Muslims fare rather poorly in Gujarat's apparatus of government. Their share of higher and lower administrative positions was 3.4 percent and 5.5 percent respectively. Most of the Muslims tend to work in the transport department, presumably as drivers.[3] Abusalesh Shariff, a member of the committee, believes that much of the government and public sector employment happened before Modi took over, but this could not be verified.

An analysis by Arvind Panagariya and Vishal More of the five-yearly national surveys based on large samples showed that poverty among Gujarati Muslims increased slightly in the five years to 2009-10 to 37.6 percent despite the peace dividend. It was unchanged among urban Muslims and slightly up in their rural communities during this period. These surveys also show that poverty among Gujarati Muslims was quite sticky; it fell by just five percentage points over the fifteen years to the end of the last decade, compared to 16 percentage points decline among Hindus.[4] Their analysis of a subsequent survey based on thin samples shows such a steep decline in Gujarati Muslim poverty that it strains credulity.

Modi can go to vexatious lengths to uphold his principle of 'justice for all and appeasement of none.' Education has both personal and social benefits; an illiterate person imposes intangible costs on society. Modi acknowledged this in a speech at Becharaji in September 2002. A 'madrasa-going child,' was 'deprived of primary

---

[3] Sachar Committee Report, 2006: Share of Muslims in Gujarat's population: according to 2001 Census was 9.1 percent. Share of higher state government posts 3.4 percent, lower posts 5.5 percent. Higher posts in education department 1.7 percent, home 5.6 percent, health 2.2 percent and transport 9.4 percent. Share of lower posts in transport department was 16.3 percent.

[4] Arvind Panagariya of Columbia University and Vishal More. Poverty by Social, Religious & Economic Groups in India and its Largest States 1993-94 to 2011-12. Poverty among Gujarati Muslims was 42.7 percent in 1993-94, 36.5 percent in 2004-05 and 37.6 percent in 2009-10. The corresponding figures for Gujarati Hindus: 38.2, 32.7 and 21.9.

education' and hence is a 'burden on the state,' he said.⁵ That was a rant against the Muslim community not a call to betterment.

The rate of literacy among Gujarati Muslims was higher than Hindus as per the 2001 census. A break-up by religion was not available for the last one. In the last big sample survey, fewer Muslims than Hindus said they were illiterate.⁶ But they also tend to drop out early. While 78 percent enrolled in schools at last count, more than half of them quit school by the age of fifteen. To encourage them to stay on, the central government instituted a pre-matriculation scholarship of about a thousand rupees a year for those with annual family income of less than Rs 1 lakh. Fifty-five thousand scholarships were offered to Gujarati Muslim students. The state government's tab was just Rs 1.25 cr a year. But Modi's government refused to implement it. The Gujarat High court ruled that the scheme fell in the category of 'affirmative action' and could not be regarded as religious 'reservation'. After exhausting all the appeals in the high court and the Supreme Court over four years, the government lost the case. It has been forced to implement the scholarship, but has made its reluctance felt. A school in Motera, near Ahmedabad's Sardar Patel stadium that caters to Muslim children from daily-wage earning families, says it had applied for 500 scholarships in September 2013. Till two months before close of the academic year it had neither got a response nor money.

Modi makes the scholarships seem sinister. He insists that 'religion-based reservations would ultimately break the country.'⁷ But the Gujarat government has been offering the central government's post-matric scholarships to minority students! On two post-matric

---

⁵ Manoj Mitta, *The Fiction of Fact-finding,* HarperCollins Publishers India, 2014.
⁶ NSSO 2009-10: 26.8 percent of Muslims and 27.4 percent of Hindus said they were not literate.
⁷ 'Religion-based reservation will break the counry,' www.narendramodi.in. Accessed on 9 March, 2014.

scholarships for 24,000 Muslim students, the department of social justice and empowerment says nearly Rs 13 cr were spent.[8]

Until the eve of the Lok Sabha elections, the Modi administration ignored Gujarat's Islamic heritage in tourism promotion campaigns. Ahmedabad was founded in the fifteenth century by Sultan Ahmed Shah. The city has many Islamic monuments of tourist interest like Sarkhej Roza, Jama Masjid, Bhadra Fort, the Shaking Minarets and Sidi Sayed Mosque (whose *jali* or stone lattice window with a tree motif is a symbol of the city). The rest of the state is also rich in historic Islamic curiosities. But they were all missing from Amitabh Bachhan's '*Khushboo* Gujarat *ki,*' campaign urging rest of Indians to spend a few days in Gujarat (*kuch din guzaro* Gujarat *mein*). His rap compositions for pilgrimage sites ignored Gujarat's religious diversity. Five years after the start of the campaign and before the general elections, the government made promotionals on two of the city's Islamic monuments with an eye on the Muslim vote — Sarkhej Roza and the Jama Masjid.[9] The film on Jama Masjid was called '*Mandir se Masjid tak*' a walk from the city's Akshardham temple to the famed mosque.

Such opportunism was very much on display in the run up to the elections. Modi made a courtesy call on the spiritual leader of the Dawoodi Bohras, the late Syedna Mohammed Burhanuddin, and inaugurated their trade exposition in Ahmedabad. The *Sadbhavana* or harmony missions and fasts went on for six months

---

[8] This was in 2012-13. The BCK-81E, scholarship pays Rs 380 a month to minority students in classes eleven and twelve or equivalent technical courses if they are in hostels. For day scholars the scholarship is Rs 230 a month. The BCK 82 A merit-cum-means scholarship pays minority community students pursuing professional degrees Rs,1,000 a month for ten months if staying in hostels and Rs 500 a month for ten months if they are day scholars. In both cases tuition and admission fees are reimbursed subject to caps. See website of Director, Developing Castes Welfare, Department of Social Justice and Empowerment, Gandhinagar.

[9] *Khushboo* Gujarat *Ki* turns spotlight on State's Islamic Architecture, *Indian Express*, 6 February, 2014.

till February 2012. It was a reach out to Sunni Muslims. However, in the assembly elections that year Modi did not nominate a single Muslim candidate. In the subsequent local by-elections, twenty-four Muslim candidates won on BJP tickets in Muslim-dominated Salaya town in Jamnagar district, but voter turnout there was the lowest in the state. The polls did not indicate healing or reconciliation. The government also declined to restore or pay compensation for over 500 Muslim shrines and tombs pulled down during the riots, including that of Wali Mohammed Wali, a revered Sufi saint. The Supreme Court had to compel it.

For ten years Modi not only ignored Muslims but also mocked them. He called the relief camps for riot affected persons baby-producing centres. Soon after the riots, he launched the *Gaurav Yatra* as if the murder of hundreds of citizens was a matter of honour. With alacrity he dissolved the Assembly and advanced the elections by one year to reap the harvest of communal fervour. When the Election Commission did not agree to his timetable in view of the unsettled conditions Modi pointedly referred to the Chief Election Commissioner by full Christian name as if that was a factor in the decision.

Modi makes much of good governance but can governance devoid of justice be good? A book by Manoj Mitta, *'The Fiction of Fact-finding, Modi and Godhra,'* published on the eve of the 2014 Lok Sabha raises uncomfortable questions. Based on reports of committees and commissions that probed riot violence, and court orders and judgments, it reveals the extent of the cover-up. The book shows how the Nanavati Commission set up by the Gujarat government and the Special Investigation Team (SIT) constituted by the Supreme Court were keen to exonerate, not ferret out the truth. It reveals that the conduct of the police was such that it could not but imply complicity. It questions the 'clean chit' given by a Gujarat magistrate to Modi on the basis of the SIT's final report.

A vigilant Supreme Court could have secured justice for the riot victims but it eludes them because of its lax monitoring of the SIT.

Here are some of the issues the book raises: (a) Why did Modi declare without evidence that the burning of the Sabarmati Express coach carrying *karsevaks* was a terror attack, which it was not? (b) Why were the fifty-four burnt bodies of *karsevaks* handed over to a leader of the Vishwa Hindu Parishad, or he was allowed to accompany them, when the same organization had organised a *bandh* and its members had taken part in reprisals the following day (28 February, 2002). Should not the bodies have been kept in a government mortuary till the next of kin claimed them? Why were the bodies brought to a hospital outside Ahmedabad? (c) How could Modi not know about the massacre at Ahmedabad's Gulberg Society (sixty-nine killed) till well past the event when he had held a meeting of officials and a press conference at a venue nearby? Why did he not punish the police officers who had kept him in the dark, though they had seen mobs milling at Gulberg. (d) Why was a police officer transferred promptly after preventing a madrasa with a few hundred students from being torched? (e) Why were state police and prosecutors reluctant to use cell phone call data records to pin down the whereabouts of rioters? One statistic is telling: of the 4,252 carnage cases booked in the state, Mitta finds magistrates accepting police reports for closing half of them — 2,215. (These were subsequently reopened on Supreme Court orders and more than a thousand police officers were arrested).[10] Societal prejudice was reinforced by the state.

The brazenness of the Gujarat administration compelled the National Human Rights Commission to inveigh on behalf of the victims. The Supreme Court moved some of the egregious cases of mass murder out of the state for prosecution. Vinay Sitapati, a lawyer and PhD candidate at Princeton University estimates the

---

[10] Aakar Patel, Modi, Sack Yourself, *Tribune*, June 30, 2012.

conviction rate in riot cases where the Supreme Court stepped in, the witnesses were protected by central police and the trials happened in Maharashtra, was 39 percent.[11] When he asked a senior Gujarat police official for statistics on the conviction rates for riot crimes tried within the state, he was told, 'we do not keep separate records of riot cases,' despite Supreme Court guidelines. He says legal researcher Pritarani Jha and others at the Centre for Equity Studies have estimated on the basis of serial Right to Information filings that the conviction rate for such cases was 5 percent. Minister Maya Kodnani and VHP leader Babu Bajrangi were convicted because the state government was kept out of the process. But he also finds fault with the NGOs who took up the cause of the riot victims. When the 'get Modi' strategy was going nowhere, they should have changed tack, he says, and gone after those who actually murdered, raped and burned. The riot machinery remains intact.

Gulberg Society stands forlorn today, indifferent to the bustle outside. Municipal garbage bins, cleared of refuse, are parked at the entrance, the ground blackened by ooze from putrefying organic matter. The houses, a mix of one and three-storeyed buildings — are unoccupied and slowly crumbling. The un-pruned trees and undergrowth are reclaiming them. Muslim hawkers rest in the verandahs at noon time. Dogs have moved into the houses; they break into fits of angry barking on spying a stranger. The place fills one with overwhelming sadness.

On the fringes of the city, off the highway to Mumbai, and at the foot of a hillock of municipal refuse, are a row of tenements, called Citizen Nagar. The name is a political statement. The Islamic Relief Centre of the Jamaat-i-Islami has been active here in helping people rebuild their lives. In monsoons the slush from the dump washes into the lanes up to the door steps. A chimney spews black smoke as workers try to salvage things of value by burning scrap material.

---

[11] Reading the cleanchit, Indian Express, 3 February, 2014.

Thirty kids sit listlessly on the floor of an *anganwadi* itching to break free. They are not supposed to step out till their parents arrive to fetch them post-noon. There is talk of two kids who went missing found murdered. The *anganwadi* caretaker's family had a furniture business before the riots. She lost all. She gets about a thousand rupees a month from the government as rent and electricity charges. Children are given snacks twice a day. They come for the food.

~

The communal divide was a reality in Gujarat even before Modi took over. The riots have widened it. On way from Ahmedabad airport to Gandhinagar for an official appointment, I break into a conversation with Mohammed Ali Saiyad, 48, who has been driving a taxi since the age of seventeen and now owns one. His brother had to vacate an apartment in Chhota Chiloda, on the outskirts of the city. Employed as an electrician with a private airline he had bought a two-room set for Rs 14 lakh. But when he got possession after eight years and moved in, he was forced out within a month or so. The owners' association said he could rent it out, but not himself stay. Saiyad suggested moving court, but his brother had no stomach for the hassles. That is how it is here, says Saiyad. 'Gujaratis do not sell to Mohemedans and Mohemedans do not sell to Gujaratis.'

The riots have made Muslims conscious of their identity. They are not fading away. Instead they are becoming visible. The *hijab* may be ridiculed as a body bag that inoculates the wearer from outside influences but for Juveria Putawala, it is a dress which is 'earning respect for us.' Far from constricting her, she finds freedom in it. 'We can move around with this anywhere.'

Putawala is the trustee of a girls' school in the Old City. The trust was formed after the 2001 earthquake. It does not take government support so it can set the curriculum. In addition to mathematics, science, English, Gujarati and social science, Arabic and the Koran are taught. Principal Zaheda Desai emphasizes moral values, which could be code for dull docility. She and Juveria are young and speak fluent English. 'Muslims are assertive, they have more confidence,' says Desai.

At the school, little girls wear hoods that cover their necks, over *salwar-kameezes*. A board tells men to keep off. For Lakdawala standing out is akin to being cut off from the rest of society. The Muslim community is torn between the proponents of sticking out and blending in.

Prejudice has seeped through all levels of the administration. Lakdawala says the government is reluctant to add schools in Muslim dominated areas of Ahmedabad like Juhapura and Bombay Hotel despite the pressure of population. Of fifty-six lakh beneficiaries of Kalyan Mela doles for the poor, he says, just 1.5 percent were Muslim, far short of their 9 percent share of population. Local officials refer to lists of poor Muslims to deny below-poverty level ration cards. For Lakdawala these are proof of the state abdicating its responsibility to citizens. His intention is not to fan disaffection, but to draw attention to its causes so as to scotch it.

Wherever the state is folding up, Islamic trusts are rolling in. At the Motera stadium, they have taken over a school that caters to 650 children of daily wage workers, a third of them girls. It is a private school and gets no government support till class eight, the ostensible reason being the presence of municipal schools in the vicinity. Parents prefer the school because its fees are nominal. Text books, sandals, school bags, uniforms and note books are given free. The standard of education is said to be better. There are weekly tests; trust officers make random checks. Teachers sign-in with biometric readers; CCTV cameras keep a watch on them.

Education is the refuge of oppressed communities. An unintended consequence of the riots is the Muslim emphasis on education.

Before the riots there were thirty community-run schools. Since then, 800 educational trusts have sprung up, according to Lakdawala. Some are run by fundamentalist sects like the Tabligi Jamaat. They impose their own codes of behaviour. Schools have become monocultural. They reflect divides in society. There is little interaction between communities. Prejudices get hardened when not chipped away by the spray of daily cross-community meetings.

Modi's own reach out suggests that Muslims (and liberals) should adopt a twin-track strategy. Pursue justice resolutely, while engaging with Modi. As chief minister of Gujarat, Modi could swim with one kind of fish. But in the larger Indian lake he is having to reach out to others. Modi's Hindutva convictions built up over the better part of sixty-three years are not lightly held. But engagement with Muslims made necessary by electoral compulsions will hopefully result in a change of attitude. Even BJP leader L K Advani tried to soften his hard line image by re-discovering Pakistan founder Mohammad Ali Jinnah's secularism. Modi's speech at the Muslim business meet (quoted at beginning of this chapter) echoed Jinnah's to the Pakistan Constituent Assembly: 'You are free; you are free to go to your temples, you are free to go to your mosques or to any other place of worship...You may belong to any religion or caste or creed — that has nothing to do with the business of the State.'

7. Commerce Without Care?

The often made accusation that Modi privileges material progress over human development is not grounded in facts. Gujarat under Modi has strived to catch up with its developed peers in social indicators but it has a legacy to overcome.

The 'national' education summit at Gandhinagar in January 2014 was a grand affair. About a 100 university vice-chancellors and directors of education were present. There were representatives from eighty-four institutes worldwide. Among the invitees were 1500 professors and teachers and 3000 students, 200 of them from forty countries. Collaboration in design studies, and Modi's national profile, had brought the Italian ambassador over for the third time in a year. Among the speakers was Delhi University's Vice-chancellor, the redoubtable Dinesh Singh, who had forced a change in the degree course against stout opposition from teachers and students. The cavernous Mahatma Mandir was packed. Modi paid homage to ideology and railed against the British educationist Lord Macaulay for 'assaulting' India's traditional structure of knowledge and 'sapping its inner energy.' He then held forth on his vision for higher education.

Even those who are not habitual critics could ask whether the extravaganza was another example of Modi using state resources for self-glorification. Even if the scale was necessary, was the timing, at the cusp of political change, right? Were there not frugally-engineered ways to make the state's capital region, a higher education hub, like Bangalore, Delhi and Pune?

'It is just propaganda,' said Sukhdev Patel, who was engaged in schooling salt-pan workers for more than two decades before leading the state unit of a party that seeks to be an 'alternative and not a substitute' to existing ones. 'There is no seriousness at all.' Patel cited Gujarat's drop in rank from twelve to twenty-eight among thirty-five states and union territories in the annual national-level audit of schools, and the lack of toilets and drinking water in an Ahmedabad school catering to over 2000 students, as proof.[1]

Gujarat's educational and health attainments were out of alignment with its economic achievements. Tamil Nadu, which is as industrialized, is a model in the delivery of public services. Cutting across political parties there is a commitment to welfare. Tamil Nadu's health services are the best in the country. The manner in which its public hospitals stock and replenish medicines has become a template for others. Tamil Nadu was a pioneer in providing school lunches. Chief Minister Kumarasami Kamraj decreed free education till high school in 1960s. Its system of supplying subsidized cereals is praised for coverage and efficiency. This is reason enough to mock the 'Gujarat model'. 'Economic growth has taken place,' under Modi said Hanif Lakdawala, a psychiatrist, who organizes community health services for Ahmedabad's slum residents, 'but development has not taken place.'

~

---

[1] (a) In National University of Education Planning and Administration's (NUEPA) annual audit, the composite score of Gujarat's primary schools fell from twelve to twenty-eight in 2012-13. In the previous eight years the rank had swung between seven and eighteen. The composite rank for primary and upper primary combined was eighteen and that of only upper primary schools had moved from eight to fourteen.
(b) The school without water and toilets was at Danilimda and catered to residents of Bombay Hotel, a Muslim-dominated sprawl.

Gujarat neglected education. Successive governments did so because there was little pressure from parents. Studious children were assumed to be bookish with little talent for advancement in life. That is yesterday's story. Advances in information and communications technology, the transformation of southern Indian cities as software services hubs, the resultant makeover of India's image, the boom in financial services, the demand for knowledge workers and their fancy earnings, have made Gujarat realize the value of education.

The drive to enroll children in schools began as a central government initiative called district primary education programme funded by British and Dutch agencies and the World Bank. The state's campaign, followed in 1997-98. Sudhir Mankad, who was the education secretary recalls approaching the chief secretary for funds to add about 10,000 classrooms and recruit double that number of teachers. When that request was less than half-way met, the department had to think creatively. Teachers were recruited on contract. These were as qualified as the regular ones, but paid about half the salary. The contracts were for five years, at the end of which they could be considered for permanent appointment. The practice was challenged in courts but stood the test of legality. Pre-fabricated structures slashed classroom building time. Only the foundation and floor were laid on site. The rest was assembled. The walls and roofs were initially of pre-cast concrete and then of hardened plastic filled with a cement mix.

Under chief minister Keshubhai Patel, a vision document for the social sector was drawn up. Kerala was chosen as the benchmark for health, nutrition, literacy, education and gender development. In 2004, two academicians, working outside government, gave Gujarat's first development report with quality of life rankings. It told the state to focus on tribal and slum clusters. The thrust on schooling is quite evident. In 2003, the government began the annual Kanya Kelavani (girl education) and Shala Praveshotsav (school admission festival) drive in which ministers and officials, cutting across departments participated. Parents were encouraged to send children, especially females, to school. Children were received in schools in a festive, welcoming atmosphere. 'Let us regard every child as a celebrity,' says Modi. In the past ten years, the number of government schools imparting primary education has more than doubled to a little short of 34,000, and their share in the total number of schools is very high. Kerala, which is celebrated for its social indicators, particularly education, is dominated by private schools. They have a two-thirds share there, because of the initiatives of its religious communities. In Tamil Nadu also, private schools have a third share.

In Gujarat, five in every six schools used to be government owned for much of the past decade. That is changing, and quite dramatically too, of late. In just one year, 1,500 private schools were added, taking their total to a tad short of 9,000, and their share to a fifth of the total. This may be a reflection of the quality of teaching in public schools, the profitability of schooling as a business, and the Muslim community taking autonomous action to counter institutionalized discrimination.

Improvement in access is also suggested by other measures. More upper primary schools have been established narrowing the numbers gap with primary schools. The retention ratio, or percentage of children staying in, was in the nineties at last count. The numbers transiting to upper primary were not far off levels in Karnataka and Tamil Nadu.

According to the last census, 79 percent of Gujarat's population aged above seven years could read and write without necessarily receiving formal education. That places it eighteenth in the list, or about midway in national rankings. At first glance this looks quite unsatisfactory. But Gujarat is a tad below Tamil Nadu; Andhra and Karnataka are worse off. It is within an arms' length of Maharashtra in literacy rate. Of course, it will have to really sweat to bridge the gap with Kerala, but then that state had a historical head start.

While levels are important, smart change over time as in Gujarat reflects government's and society's effort.[2]

There has been a ten percentage point improvement in Gujarat's literacy rate from the previous census. Among females the jump was higher. National school audits certify that facilities in Gujarat's schools are improving. The contribution of another drive called Gunotsav, begun in 2009, may have contributed. Under this 'Quality Festival' officials assess schools on various parameters for three days every November. The proportion of schools getting a score of at least six on ten was 44 percent in 2011. Only a few schools do not have girls' toilet (though there is no reason why all should not. Also, there is a gap between availability and usability.). Drinking water is provided in most schools. There are three lakh teachers. That is one for every thirty pupils in government schools, comparable to Tamil Nadu's ratio. Meals are provided in almost all government and state-aided schools but a fifth do not get them cooked on site. These are possibly in cities, in which case, like in Delhi and Puducherry, it makes better hygienic sense to source the meals from automated centralized kitchens.

In terms of learning, Gujarat's students are as worse off as those in say Maharashtra or Tamil Nadu, though that is little consolation. According to NGO Pratham's latest benchmark Annual Survey of Education Report (ASER), after eight years of schooling, only 35 percent of rural Gujarat students could do division, the same as in Maharashtra. Tamil Nadu students did somewhat better. Only 18 percent of class three rural students in Gujarat's government schools could at least do subtraction, the same as in the other two states. Half of class five students of Gujarat could not read a class

---

[2] Gujarat's 2011 literacy rate was 79 percent, a ten percentage point gain over the previous census. The rate for males was 87 percent, an eight percentage point gain, and for women 71 percent, an advance of thirteen percentage points. Tamil Nadu's literacy rate was 80 percent, that of Maharashtra 83 percent. Andhra's was 68 percent and Karantaka's 76 percent.

two text. In Maharashtra 40 percent could not and in Tamil Nadu, 68 percent! Now that access has been assured, the challenge is to ensure that schooling actually results in learning.

In secondary and higher secondary, that is till class twelve, Gujarat has the same proportion of schools as Tamil Nadu and more than Maharashtra. Their spread is skewed in favour of rural areas. The representation of dalits and tribals in schools is in line with their slice of the population. The net enrolment ratio however is quite low. Only 42 percent of students in secondary schools are of the right age; this dips by nearly half at the next stage. In Tamil Nadu, six out of ten students at the secondary level are likely to be of the right age. There is a dip at the next stage but not as pronounced as in Gujarat. Gujarat also lags behind Maharashtra and Tamil Nadu in gender party. There are seven to eight girls for every ten boys in class ten and twelve.[3]

Gujarat is now gearing up to catch up in higher education. According to an annual survey done by the Confederation of Indian Industry for the Planning Commission, at last count Gujarat ranked eighth in the country in number of colleges (1,815). It had a gross enrolment rate of twenty-one, compared to the national average of nineteen. Tamil Nadu which ranks first on this score was way ahead at thirty-three.

Though Modi speaks of Gujarat as a paradise of private enterprise its higher education system is not as privatized as in the southern states — not yet. Unaided private colleges have a 40 percent share. Most students enroll in government colleges or those aided by it. In Tamil Nadu, nine in ten colleges are private and their share of enrolments is about as high.

Modi is keen on making Gujarat a knowledge hub. A variety of universities — petroleum, agriculture, hospitality, defence and

---

[3] NUEPA state report card for 2012-13.

security, Sanskrit, and yoga, have sprung up. Hopefully, these will not be mere real estate plays. Some of his loyal officials have been accommodated in these sinecures post-retirement. The number of engineering seats, according to the state's economic review, has seen a four-fold increase in eight years to 56,000. There are as many diploma seats in the discipline as well. Engineering seems to have caught the students' fancy. Skill development is being emphasized to prepare students for manufacturing jobs. At the 'national summit' mentioned at the beginning of this chapter, Modi told educators to give aptitude certificates instead of character certificates. 'Take the kids to manufacturing plants,' he said. He suggested that the school system be made flexible enough for students to move seamlessly between campuses and workplaces so that they can continually hone their skills and acquire qualifications on the go. Modi wants to make the state's capital region a knowledge zone. Some institutional mechanisms have been put in place to achieve this. He is keen on getting foreign investment as well unlike his party which opposed a central bill to allow the entry of foreign universities.

~

In December 2013 the Gujarat government got to hear some shocking news. Its 'model' Chiranjeevi Yojana programme to boost hospital deliveries and reduce deaths of poor mothers while giving birth, and that of new-borns, did not make a difference that was 'statistically significant', said a widely-publicized report. True, there was an increase in hospital deliveries across the state but that could not be attributed to the programme which the government had launched in five tribal districts in 2006 and across the state the following year.

The evaluation was done by researchers with strong credentials. They came from UK's Duke University, the Rand Corporation, Stanford University, Stanford Medical School and Delhi-based

Sambodhi, a private research organization.[4] There were other startling findings. Fifty-four percent of mothers interviewed said they got no relief from complications like premature delivery, prolonged and obstructed labour, excessive bleeding, hypertension, fever and incontinence after availing of the scheme. There was not much difference in their spending on hospital deliveries either, said Manoj Mohanan, assistant professor of Public Policy at Duke University and lead researcher.

Chiranjeevi Yojana was hailed as a model and had won the *Wall Street Journal's* award for innovation. The Gujarat government's prestige was riding on it. For every thousand live births, its death rate among infants in 2005-6 was fifty-seven and that of mothers 3.89. It had vowed to bring this rate down to thirty and one respectively by 2010. The key was to persuade poor women to give birth in hospitals and not at home, where the risk of lethal infection is high.

But there were not enough obstetricians and gynaecologists in the rural health set up. Those employed by the government preferred urban postings; in rural areas there were just seven obstetricians serving a population of thirty-two million. Government pay scales did not match up to earnings from private practice and the government had disallowed it for its staff.

After consulting with management experts, an NGO working with women, and a German development agency, health official Amarjit Sinha decided to enlist the services of qualified private medical practitioners who had access to maternity facilities. The empanelled doctors would be paid a fixed amount (Rs 179,000) for one hundred deliveries, including not more than seven Caesarian sections. This was to discourage unnecessary surgeries. The ratio was not arbitrary; it was based on medical data. Payment for

---

[4] Effect of Chiranjeevi Yojana on institutional deliveries and neonatal and maternal outcomes in Gujarat, India; a difference-in-differences analysis. Bulletin of the World Health Organization, 9 December, 2013.

transportation of mothers, and an allowance for attendants was included in the package.

In 2009, Sinha along with other researchers reported encouraging results in a bulletin of the World Health Organization.[5] After scaling up the programme to the entire state, 865 obstetricians had enrolled, he said. They had performed about 175,000 deliveries till end of March the previous year. Caesarians were six percent of the total; this was less than what was allowed, but double the number observed among the poor. Post Chiranjeevi, there was a 27 percent increase in hospital deliveries among the poor, a 60 percent reduction in infant deaths and 90 percent fall in maternal mortality, Sinha reported. This was the first practical experience of providing medical care on a large-scale to the poor in partnership with private practitioners, he said. It demonstrated that if the government was willing to pay reasonable fees, social health insurance could be rapidly scaled up in private partnership without involving donors and insurance companies (which had been discouraged by the low fees).

Previous studies had looked at results only in hospitals which were providing this service. Mohanan's team looked at the complete below poverty level criteria and population groups that delivered during that time. 'If the programme leads to more people using it, you should see that difference over time but we found a trend that looks similar to the one before the Yojana. We had come to the table to find a programme so successful and impressive in ambition was not being used by half the people who were eligible for it,' Mohanan told the *Times of India*.

Inaccurate classification of below poverty level people was the reason why the campaign's success was misread, Mohanan says. There are problems of inclusion and exclusion, that is, those that

---

[5] Providing skilled birth attendants and emergency obstetric care to the poor through partnership with private sector obstetricians in Gujarat, India. Bulletin of the World Health Organization, 2009. Amarjit Singh, Dileep V Mavlankar and others.

were indeed very poor and should be in the BPL list were not included, and those that were not, were. As a result, those not eligible were claiming Chiranjeevi Yojana benefits. Hospitals may also have falsified data. Reports that they charged extra from Yojana patients may have discouraged the intended beneficiaries.

What puzzled the researchers the most was the little or no difference which the Yojana made on cost of hospital delivery. 'At the end of the day, the private sector is the private sector. You need a monitoring system to check the extra costs that hospitals might be charging and to ensure proper implementation. The second is the costing. Is Rs 1,600 enough reimbursement to the hospital? I don't know how they came up with the number,' said Mohanan. He added that the success of the scheme needed to be scrutinized further before other states decided to adopt it.[6]

State auditors had also pointed out that private doctors were lukewarm to the programme. In its 2011 report, the Comptroller and Auditor General found in ninety-three, or 40 percent, of 231 talukas, private doctors had not enlisted for the scheme. Mothers were not given transport charges or were short-paid. There was also no process to verify whether doctors had performed the deliveries they claimed; so there was a possibility of fraud. There were reports of doctors charging extra from the patients or giving them less attention than for those who paid the full fees. Another study in Surat district said doctors did not join the scheme in rural areas where it was most needed, or turned away complicated cases.

It would be wrong to see this episode as yet another example of hype running ahead of reality. The sincerity of the officials cannot be doubted. Design changes will be needed or a change in the way the scheme is implemented.

---

[6] Gujarat's Maternal Health Scheme is a Failure, Padmaparna Ghosh, *Times of India*, 30 December, 2013.

The state will also need to revive the public health system. Reliance on the private sector would be a mistake. It can at best complement. It is not an alternative. Delhi's experience with providing land at concessional rates to private hospitals on condition that they reserve 10 percent of the beds for poor patients and give them free treatment has been very discouraging. Hospitals flout court orders and government directives without any fear of punishment. The regulatory mechanism has been found wanting in integrity and commitment.

Gujarat's neglect of the public health system shows up. Only about a 100 primary health centres were added over a ten year period. In Tamil Nadu, the 2014 budget made a provision for much more than that number to be built in just one year. This will take the total to more than what is minimally required. In Tamil Nadu there is no shortfall of other rural facilities like community centres either. The number of doctors at primary health centres is double the minimum so that they can be available round the clock. During a visit to Dharmapuri, a district adjoining Karnataka and regarded as backward, one found people vouching for the quality of service in government centres. Private doctors said they were losing patients. To cope with the reluctance of specialists to join the rural health system, the Tamil Nadu government trains graduate doctors in specializations like anesthesia, obstetrics and radiology so that they can deal with medical emergencies.

The cost for its people will be high if Gujarat does not reinvent the healthcare system. Its urban infant mortality rate (twenty-four per thousand) is the same as that of rural Tamil Nadu. If Modi wants rural Gujarat to enjoy urban standards, he will have to slash the death rate of new borns — a metaphor for development — currently at forty-five per thousand (and thirty-eight for the state as a whole). That will be the true test of his style of governance.

8. MODI ON KASHMIR AND FOREIGN POLICY

On these issues, can Modi's actions match his roar?

'*F*riends, till when will these double standards last?'

At the Lalkaar rally in Jammu in December 2013, Narendra Modi touched on the sensitive subject of Article 370, which gives special status to Jammu & Kashmir. Repeal of the article is an immutable demand of the BJP, which it downplays when expedient. Modi said the article has become a 'shield' fortified with 'communal jewels,' to fend off discussion on whether it has helped development of the state and the welfare of its people. Modi reminded the audience that Prime Minister Jawaharlal Nehru had said the article would 'fade away.' Because of J&K's special status, people were being denied the benefit of reservations which rest of Indians enjoyed. 'Friends, till when will these double standards last?' Modi asked. 'This politics of discrimination, the politics of separation, it has just destroyed this nation. If development has to be done, then the politics of integration will work and only that will let us grow!'

Modi said J&K had become dependent on the centre though it could thrive, given its hydro-electric resources, herbal abundance, scenic landscapes and mineral wealth. Modi invoked the magic charm of development: 'Friends, how would it be if in place of a separate state, there prevailed the dreams of a super state! You tell me, do you want a separate state or a super state?'

Modi offered the Vajpayee formula of addressing the state's concerns with *insaniyat* (humanity), *jammuriyat* (democracy) and *Kashmiriyat* (or the tradition of religious tolerance). In a January 2014 blog, he said the army's presence in J&K was necessary till Pakistan dismantled the infrastructure of terrorism and stopped supporting terrorism in the Valley.[1]

~

Strong economy is driver of an effective foreign policy.

Delivering the Nani Palkhivala memorial lecture on 'India and the World' in Chennai in October, 2013, Modi said, 'I believe a strong economy is driver of an effective foreign policy and national security strategy.' (Palkhivala was India's ambassador to the United States and a Constitutional expert who defended fundamental rights.)

Reading out from a prepared text in English, Modi appreciated Prime Minister Atal Behari Vajpayee's policy of combining *Shakti* with *Shanti*. In May 1999, Vajpayee had braved international sanctions, conducted five nuclear tests, declared India to be a nuclear weapons state but renounced first use.

While India was perceived as big brother because of its size, it should be sensitive to their concerns without being perceived as weak. Pakistan should be pinned down in the global arena for its support to terrorism. But Modi did not spell out how he would deal

---

[1] In October 2010, the Home Ministry appointed a three person committee, comprising Editor Dileep Padgaonkar, Professor Radha Kumar and retired bureaucrat M M Ansari. In a report, a year later, they said the state's distinctive status must be upheld, and a Constitutional Committee must be appointed to review the extent to which, central laws applied to the state after having diluted its special status. Contrary to what Modi said, caste and tribal reservations are available in J&K.

with terrorist training camps in Pakistan-held Kashmir, another Mumbai-type terror attack, or get Pakistan to punish its nationals involved in those attacks. Nor was there clarity on the exchange of enclaves along the India-Bangladesh border, or on Sir Creek, a disputed stretch of water which separates the Rann of Kutch from Pakistan's Sindh province. In September 2012, Prime Minister Manmohan Singh had said Sir Creek was 'doable' but Modi had written to him to drop negotiations with Pakistan.

Modi represents a brand of Asian nationalism kindled by China's rise, says a commentator.[2] In his Chennai lecture, Modi chided the Manmohan Singh government for its weak response to Chinese incursions, though his attitude to China is unlikely to be different from his predecessor's, except in forceful articulation.[3] He is expected to pay close attention to improvement of border infrastructure, the economic development of the North-East, and especially of Arunachal Pradesh. Settling the border dispute might be tough, but a right-wing government will be able to sell it to people better.[4]

Modi wanted states to be involved in building bridges with countries they had historical ties with, like Tamil Nadu with South East Asia or Gujarat with East Africa. He wanted every state to assign a certain number of their teachers to learn the language of their partner country.

Like the oil cartel, Opec, India should head a club of countries with strong solar radiation, conduct research in solar energy and reduce dependence on oil. Modi believes that tourism could be a foreign policy instrument. 'Terrorism divides but tourism unites.'

---

[2] The World of Narendra Abe, Sanjaya Baru, *Indian Express*, 27 February, 2014
[3] ibid
[4] UPA II's National Security Advisor Shiv Shanker Menon said there was broad agreement that the border dispute should be resolved without displacing settled populations. There were 'critical differences' on the framework for settlement. Delineation of the border would be the last step.

9. What Drives Modi?

Modi's rise is a marvel of India's democracy. If he gets the mandate, Modi can unite Indians in joint endeavour for national greatness, or like leaders of neighbouring Sri Lanka and Pakistan, let loose atavistic passions and tear the social compact that has bound the country together for more than sixty-five years.

Power undoubtedly drives Modi. It impels him inexorably like a jet engine. His pursuit of it has been sustained, his desire singular, his claim so forceful he seems deserving of it. There is no greater immorality than to occupy a chair one cannot fill. Modi could have uttered those words. He gives no quarter. When sounded out for a power-sharing arrangement with Keshubhai Patel in 2001, he rebuffed the deal: 'You keep him, I am either going to be fully responsible for Gujarat, or not at all,' he told BJP leaders.[1] In 2012 he forced Nitin Gadkari into a humiliating capitulation by compelling him to drop an RSS *pracharak* in charge of the Uttar Pradesh assembly elections. Since Gadkari was acting on the dictates of the RSS, Modi was also questioning the right of the RSS to decide political appointments in the BJP that he did not approve of.

Indira Gandhi's passing away was supposed to be the end of charismatic politics. Her hold on people was so mesmerizing that she could get people elected regardless of their credentials. With total power over party and Cabinet she privileged personal loyalty

---

[1] Aditi Phadnis, *Political Profiles of Cabals and Kings*, BS Books, 2009.

over allegiance to the Constitution. India's democratic institutions crumbled under the weight of her commanding personality.

Rajiv Gandhi also acted imperiously before and during his years as Prime Minister. '(H)is unprecedented majority turned his head completely,' says socialist Madhu Limaye in his 1989 book on cabinet government in India.[2] 'No sooner had he formed his cabinet in January 1985 than he virtually put it on shelf!' The anti-defection law and the Punjab and Assam accords were signed without the Cabinet being taken into confidence. Government was run like a club. Ministers were moved around at will. An example of Gandhi's highhandedness was the sacking of his foreign secretary, a veteran with thirty-six years of experience, at a press conference.

After Prime Minister Narasimha Rao ushered in major economic reforms with a finance minister who had not been tested in the electoral battleground and without a Congress majority in Parliament the realization gained ground that governments, without towering leadership, could perform. In fact, mass appeal could be a disadvantage. Wise lightweights could achieve desirable change through negotiation and compromise because they did not pose a threat to partners. Rao had retired and was recalled after Congress won the most seats in elections that followed Rajiv Gandhi's assassination. He contested a by-election after becoming Prime Minister. Finance Minister Manmohan Singh entered the House through the Rajya Sabha.

The continuation of reforms by subsequent Prime Ministers H D Deve Gowda and Inder Kumar Gujral supported this theory. It got an endorsement when Prime Minister Atal Behari Vajpayee failed to lead his coalition to victory in 2004. Opinion polls had said he was the best prime ministerial candidate. He had a giant personality. He came across as a unifier who could cut across political lines. He was a master practitioner of coalition politics. So

---

[2] Madhu Limaye, *Cabinet Government in India*, Radiant Publishers, 1989.

assured was Vajpayee of the National Democratic Alliance's record in office that he advanced the elections confident of victory. His shock defeat to the Congress led by a rather diffident Sonia Gandhi and the anointing of the shy and withdrawing Manmohan Singh as head of government seemed to suggest that India was done with fiery orators who could move the masses.

Soon after those elections, the political commentator Pratap Bhanu Mehta said Indian politics had changed structurally and it would be difficult for powerful national leaders to emerge.[3] Parties had become loyalty-inducing machines. Emerging leaders were felled the moment their ambition crossed set limits. Regional satraps cancelled each other out; consensus-seeking neutral leaders had a greater chance at the centre, Mehta said.

'It is proving very difficult for any chief minister, or regional big boss to transcend the boundaries of their state.' Mehta's observation had largely held good. But it seems so off the mark in the light of current developments. Mehta did leave the possibility open, though. Extraordinary leaders could emerge 'under very exceptional circumstances, or by an extraordinary act of political imagination.'

If Manmohan Singh's elevation was the highpoint of non-charismatic politics, his latter term in office showed the limits of the politics of self-effacement. People did not want a leader who would walk all over them; but they do not also want one who would be walked over. Modi, his polar opposite, barged through doors which Singh opened.

Modi's emergence on the national scene is the triumph of pure Will. It is sheer ambition that has helped him surmount the odds. Singh's 'emasculated goodness' robbed him of authority. It allowed Modi to project himself as India's deliverer. Singh's reluctance to speak out made people forget his achievements: ten years of social

---

[3] Pratap Bhanu Mehta, *The End of Charisma*, Seminar, 2004.

peace, a sense of security among minorities, the empowerment of tribals through the Forest Rights Act, the fastest decline in poverty — of 140 million people — in India's history, the rise in rural incomes through schemes like employment guarantee, the highest addition of power generation capacity (Rs 53,000 MW) during the eleventh plan ending 2012, the decline in infant mortality rate from fifty-eight per thousand live births to forty-two, the rejuvenation of the rural health system, the incentivizing of urban reforms, high 6.6 percent annual growth rate for ten years, the end of India's nuclear isolation, the empowerment of citizens through right to information and an unique ID for residents to claim welfare benefits in cash. But scams, elevated and sustained inflation, weak government finances, and growth opportunities lost because of poor execution and ministers pulling in different directions, made Modi's sparkle by contrast. The dazzle blinded his many failings.

Even a charismatic leader in the current circumstances will not have the latitude of Nehru, Indira Gandhi and Rajiv. Single party dominance is unlikely. Leaders of parties anchoring ruling coalitions will have to contend with scheming colleagues and demanding allies. Their vulnerability will be inversely proportional to the own numbers they command.

Though monetary, fiscal and investment policies are decided nationally, the economic reforms of 1991 have given Indian states much more freedom to chart out their own courses of development. Chief ministers run states like prime ministers. They quash opposition within their parties and act decisively through select bureaucrats ignoring ministers and the Opposition. In Gujarat Modi is the unquestioned leader. Is he temperamentally suited to deal with the strong-willed Mulayams, Mayawatis, Jayalalithaas and Nitish Kumars?

Modi is not oblivious of the challenges. 'PM and CM are real national team,' he said during a speech in Delhi.[4] Why assume

---

[4] Modi's speech to chartered accountants in Delhi on 27 February, 2014.

that Modi's style is set in stone and he is not adaptable? Before the riots and his first Assembly election victory, Modi was quite diffident; he was wary of businessmen, says a former secretary who had held industry, investment and trade promotions posts in the state government and at the centre. 'He was a political bureaucrat,' admits a political analyst who has tracked Modi even when he was not well known. 'Muslims and secular Indians made him a mass figure.' (In other words, their disapproval of his handling of the riots brought Gujarat's voters flocking to him).

Modi is regarded as a disruptionist. Though from the RSS he does not behave like one. When deputed to the BJP, he created his own power structure. His trait of self-promotion sits ill with the RSS demand of obedience and organization before oneself. Modi has an acute understanding of people. He knows when to use people and partners and when to put them aside. His networking skills are not inconsiderable.

This makes him a consummate practitioner of power politics. But he also has commitment. A senior bureaucrat who has been closely associated with him says, 'If you do not have commitment power will not follow you.'

Modi is a committed Hindu nationalist. In *Jyotipunj*, a book he authored in 2001 in which he pays tribute to the RSS leaders who shaped him, Modi says, 'what is best in me, finest in me, is due in large part to my training with the RSS.' During the Lok Sabha elections however, he has refrained from making communal appeals. But a long-time journalist-friend of Modi's, does not expect him to dilute the RSS's 'core vision of India first, religion second' (or doing away with Constitutional privileges for minorities).

At 63, Modi is 'young' by Indian political standards. Without underplaying the odds and assuming he gets parked in South Block, Modi will not be satisfied with one term. He is a marathon player, and will want to be remembered as a leader who prefixed 'India' with 'Great'. Liberals will expect him to at least postpone divisive issues and not indulge the Hindutva ideologues. This is also what the enlightened among the corporate community, which is rooting for him, expects.

Even if he cannot win minorities over, Modi might not want to antagonize them. Playing up issues like uniform civil code, repeal of Kashmir's special status and the construction of a Ram Mandir at Ayodhya will set off social tensions and curdle the investment mood. These might be on BJP billboards for optical reasons, as items on the agenda to be achieved when the party has a clear majority. But the communalization of school text books, the amplification of the majoritarian discourse and the placement of ideologues atop universities and academic institutions might well happen. It will lull the ideologues and affirm Modi's credentials as a Hindutva icon.

On the economic front, much is expected of Modi. There is enough advice in the various reports that have been commissioned since. Liberalization began on what needs to be done; execution will be critical to achieving it. To act decisively, his government must function cohesively.

Modi will have to invest in a strong Prime Minister's Office. The PMO got a personality of its own under Indira Gandhi. The PM's secretariat as it was called acquired heft because of P N Haskar, whom Indira Gandhi drafted as her principal private secretary. It ran a parallel government, says Limaye. 'The Cabinet Secretariat became a cipher.'[5] Haksar was instrumental in the nationalization of banks and the abolition of pensions to former royals who had agreed to merge their kingdoms and estates with India.[6] These policies enabled Indira Gandhi to project herself as the messiah of the poor, and discredit party bosses known as the 'Syndicate.'

---

[5] Madhu Limaye, *Cabinet Government in India*, Radiant Publishers, 1989.
[6] Rejigging the Elephant Dance: Haksar Memorial Lecture, delivered by former RBI Governor D. Subbarao in Chandigarh, 25 November, 2011.

Prime Minister Narasimha Rao succeeded in turning around India's economic course using the opportunity afforded by the foreign exchange crisis. He named the right persons — Manmohan Singh and P Chidambaram — to the critical ministries. Importantly, in principal secretary Amar Nath Verma, he had a hands-on nuts-and-bolts official, who forced the pace of execution with detailed planning, coordination, monitoring and follow-up. Author and former corporate leader, Gurcharan Das, says Verma's office 'became a control room for implementing the reforms.' In his Thursday meetings, secretaries of economic ministries would meet and discuss strategy week after week. None of them was allowed to leave Delhi on that day, Das says. Verma would summarize the outcome and prepare the minutes. Cabinet notes would follow from them.

Prime Minister Atal Behari Vajpayee had Brajesh Mishra as principal secretary who also doubled up as National Security Adviser. The national highways programme and telecom reforms were coordinated by the PMO under him.

Manmohan Singh appointed T K A Nair to head the PMO, but it was as unempowered as the Prime Minister. It was famously unable to force the pace of preparations to the Commonwealth Games on which India had staked its prestige. Pulok Chatterjee who took over as principal secretary to the PM, when Nair retired in 2011 tried to end the policy paralysis by forcing Coal India, for instance, to assure coal supplies to power projects or arrange imports. But it took P Chidambram's return as finance minister in 2012 and the formation of the Cabinet Committee on Investment to clear about 300 projects with an investment of Rs 5 lakh cr, in the power, coal and highways sectors.

Matters do not end with cabinet approvals. India's environmental and land acquisition laws have become new instruments of the license-permit raj. Any leader who wants big investments to flow in will have to cut down the time it takes to obtain these permissions without jeopardizing the interests of forest dwellers and land owners.

The next Prime Minister will have to grapple with thorny second generation issues in labour, agriculture, infrastructure and the privatization of state enterprises in non-strategic areas. The performance of ministries will depend on the competence of ministers appointed to them. Suresh Prabhu in Vajpayee's cabinet was a charged reform-oriented power minister. But Shiv Sena chief Bal Thackerary short-circuited his tenure. B C Khanduri brought military discipline into the Golden Quadrilateral highways programme. Arun Shourie moved the telecom sector to a revenue-sharing arrangement that saw tariffs falling and mobile ownership expanding. As disinvestment minister he plucked the courage to privatize state enterprises instead of merely selling their equity in installments keeping state ownership intact. In UPA's first term, Raghuvansh Prasad Singh surprised with his performance in rural development. Kapil Sibal showed that even the low profile science and technology ministry could be elevated; he installed an early warning system for tsunamis and other natural disasters. Lalu Prasad improved railway performance and finances. Dinesh Trivedi, would have been an able successor, if Trinamool Congress chief Mamata Bannerjee's impetuosity had not felled him.

~

Here is a list of priorities for the next Prime Minister.

Restructuring of the railways will have multiplier effects on the economy. China had just 22,000 km of railways at the time of the Communist Revolution. When India became independent two years before, its network was two-and-a-half times more extensive. China has caught up since then. In the 1990s, its railways were reorganised along commercial lines. Operations were separated from policy-making. This was recommended for the Indian Railways too by the Rakesh Mohan committee in 2001, but never implemented. China's Railways are now the locomotive of its economy. They are the busiest freight carriers in the world, after US railroads, and the largest mover of passengers. They carry over three billion tons annually; Indian Railways have just crossed the one billion ton mark. Since 2008, China has built 10,000 km of high-speed track; India has none.

Admittedly, high-speed railways cost a lot and are not generally profitable. The investment in the Beijing-Shanghai line was $33 billion — more than the Three Gorges Dam. It is unlikely that it will make money. But high-speed trains have economic pay-offs. They can move large numbers quickly without the pollution load of aircraft. The development of new cities and boost to existing ones along the route can spur economic growth.

Indian Railways have been untouched by reform. They continue to function as a department of the government. Decision-making is slow and accountability to people virtually nil, despite the annual presentation of their budget in Parliament. Their services have been deteriorating and they impose a high cost on exports and domestic goods, when they should be a low-cost carrier. Three committees since 2001 have given their advice on safety and business restructuring. The next prime minister must dust those up for quick implementation. The two freight corridors of 3,300 km that connect Delhi and Ludhiana with Mumbai and Kolkata were proposed in 2005. The deadline of 2017 should be inviolate. When those lines become operational, a lot of existing capacity will be freed up for movement of passengers. Japan has proposed semi-high speed trains between Delhi and Mumbai with modifications to existing track, improved signaling and much less investment than full-fledged high speed. Quicker passenger movement, improved services and lower freight costs will help the economy like Vajpayees's highway programme. The railways can help cut down India's oil bill. A comfortable seat or berth if available on demand, will earn the next government the gratitude of people, cutting across income levels, including migrants.

The next Prime Minister must also try to denationalize the coal industry and break up Coal India, which produces 80 percent of India's coal. The industry was nationalized in two phases between 1971 and 1973. Private captive mining is allowed for the power and steel sectors.

India has the fifth largest reserves of coal but was the third largest importer in 2013.[7] About 40,000 MW of power capacity is idle for want of coal. The coal denationalization bill was introduced in 1997 but has lacked the political support for it to become law. Though coal is a central subject, the law governing mines and mineral development gives power to the states, if coal bearing areas require land acquisition. Opening a coal mine takes about ten years and about a hundred permits. A competitive coal mining industry, which does not flout environmental or safety standards, will energize the economy like never before.

The next Prime Minster should ensure that power actually flows into the 5.9 lakh villages (out of 6.3 lakh) that have been provided with an electricity connection. This will bring down the use of kerosene for lighting rural homes — and the subsidy bill. Cold storages will take off; these have not been set up in the numbers required despite capital subsidies because the cost of operating them on captive power is too high. Reduced wastage will raise farm incomes. It will increase supply and bring down inflation. Rural industries can develop, providing an alternative to farm employment. States should also be incentivized to separate the farm pump grids from the networks supplying electricity to homes and establishments. This can help conserve groundwater and control the power subsidy bill. States should be prodded to allow farmers to sell directly to buyers, whether large retailers or agro processors. There will be opposition from the *arhatiyas* or *mandi* commission

---

[7] Reuters, quoting research agency OneTeam said on 22 January, 2014 that India's coal imports had gone up by 21 percent in 2013 to 152 million tons. It quoted BP Plc assessment that India has the fifth largest reserves of coal.

agents; taking them on will be a test of the government's resolve to reform the agricultural sector.

The Goods and Services Tax (GST) will carry forward tax reforms that include a shift by states to Value Added Tax (VAT) in April 2005; the introduction of service tax and its progressive application to all but a few items; and the modification of central excise to give credit for excise paid earlier in the manufacturing process (Cenvat). GST was supposed to be applicable from 2010 but ran into political rough weather as relations between the BJP and the Congress became fraught. GST will replace Cenvat, service tax and VAT with a single tax at the centre and another at the state level. Though there is agreement on a dual tax structure, there are disagreements among states on the following: whether petroleum products and alcohol should be kept out; how will states be compensated for loss of revenue; and will levy of say, entry tax be possible. An information technology network has been set up to implement GST. States had misgivings when VAT was introduced. But revenue collection increased by 14 percent in the very first year, 21 percent the next and by 24 percent the following year. GST will be as levitating.[8]

There has been much talk about India's young population and the demographic dividend. In the past decade, there have been smart initiatives in skill development. But where are the jobs? India must raise the share of manufacturing in GDP to over 30 percent by the end of this decade. It has hovered at 16 percent for the past ten years. This is much lower than it was in fast-growing East Asian economies at our stage of development. The National Manufacturing Competitiveness Council, headed by the very capable corporate leader, V Krishmurthy, gave a strategy report in 2006. That same year the first special economic zones came up as manufacturing enclaves free of friction — infrastructural and regulatory — that frustrated activity outside them. But the

---

[8] Economic Surveys.

Communists did not allow labour laws to be relaxed while voting for the passage of SEZ legislation; the zones also became real estate grabs and ran into popular opposition.

The Economic Survey of 2012-13 had a chapter on why businesses are not creating more productive jobs. Unlike in the United States where surviving start-ups grow spectacularly, small enterprises in India are incentivized to stay small; there is no service tax for less than Rs 1 cr turnover, or no central excise duty up to Rs 1.5 cr revenue. Consequently, there are too many tiny businesses employing less than ten persons (85 percent in the apparel industry, for example); medium enterprises are near non-existent. Ninety-five percent of workers are in the informal sector or work in the formal sector without social security. It is critical, therefore, to change such perverse concessions that force entrepreneurs to break their operations into several tiny units. We also need an intermediate structure of employment (between permanent and informal) that can be made politically acceptable through fair severance packages, unemployment insurance and provision for reversal of unfair dismissals.

There is little political consensus on relaxing labour laws; both the NDA and UPA governments did little to create it. The ministers heading labour ministries have not been reformers, nor have they been political movers and shakers. None has bothered to implement the sensible Second Labour Commission recommendations of 2002, which advised that enterprises should be allowed to lay off workers partly or wholly, by paying graded compensation depending on whether downsizing is for revival of an enterprise or whether the layoffs are forced by business distress.

Since a consensus will take time to forge, the next government must (so the Survey suggests) give states the freedom to experiment and allow such flexibility in labour laws as does not conflict with central laws. There is evidence that states that have less stiff labour laws score high on labour productivity.

When governments take up projects in mission mode, they have delivered. This is how polio was eliminated in India in just sixteen years. With mass awareness and vaccination, the number of infections dropped from an estimated 500 cases *every day* before 1978, to 2,000 a year after 1995. The last case was detected on 13 January, 2011.

And here is how the next Prime Minister can add muscle to our manufacturing industry while addressing national security concerns. India is the largest arms buyer in the world. When we import armaments we export jobs. The Commerce and Industry ministry has been urging 74 percent foreign direct investment. The limit of 26 percent has brought in only $4.12 million (not billion) in FDI ever since the 'relaxation' was made in 2001. A minority stake does not persuade foreign companies to part with technology. Defence suppliers who visited India with the British Prime Minister and the French President in 2013 told the then commerce minister that they would invest if India was welcoming.

The defence ministry has not been. It believes giving control to foreign investors in joint ventures will check indigenous design and development. It is also overly protective of the eight defence public sector undertakings and forty-two ordnance factories. Perhaps it prefers to import as the cost savings resulting from local development and production do not translate into higher budget outlays. So a half-way house prevails: the cap of 26 percent will be relaxed selectively to 49 percent with approval of the Cabinet Committee on Security.

Indian industry chambers have supported the defence ministry. They privilege their own commercial interests over the nation's strategic concerns. Technology will not flow in even with higher FDI, they say, because foreign partners are answerable to their governments who wield the veto.

Fears that Indian capabilities will atrophy upon the entry of foreign suppliers are exaggerated. Indian R&D is not so weak that it cannot compete. The development of Prithvi and Agni missiles as examples of the technological distance India has travelled since the 1950s when there was no such thing as defence research in India. Where India falters is in large scale manufacturing capability. This is a reason for delay of several marquee defence projects like the main battle tank and the light combat aircraft, the other being restrictions imposed on India under international treaties to prevent the spread of missile and nuclear weapons technologies.

The Defence Research and Development Organization has built a network of 400 public and private sector supplier companies which can supply anything from rocket motors, to launchers to computers. The level of indigenization has gone up from 30 per cent in the 90s to around 55 percent. This can go up to 70 percent with some effort.

India's current year's defence budget is $40 billion at the present value of the dollar. It has been the largest arms equipment for several years now. It has a Rs 623,000 cr ($103 billion) defence modernization programme. This is sufficient inducement for foreigners to produce in India. Even if they do not part with the latest technology, they will be creating jobs. Indians will develop skills and create a strong manufacturing base for exports.

We must learn from our automobile industry. One hundred percent FDI has allowed us to export cars to tough Western markets and develop the 'frugally engineered' Nano. This is how China leverages its buying power whether to secure Boeing's manufacturing facility or to get the world's railway majors to part with technology. Gujarat has based its development model on the Chinese. If Modi becomes the next Prime Minister he must be as over-reaching as their leaders are.

❐